Knitting Fair Isle Mittens & Gloves

Knitting Fair Isle Mittens & Gloves

40 Great-Looking Designs

Carol Rasmussen Noble

LARK BOOKS
A Division of Sterling Publishing Co., Inc.
New York

EDITOR
Marcianne Miller

ART DIRECTOR
Dana Irwin

PRODUCTION
Charlie Covington

COVER DESIGN
Barbara Zaretsky

PHOTOGRAPHY
Evan Bracken

EDITORIAL ASSISTANCE
Delores Gosnell

PRODUCTION ASSISTANT
Shannon Yokeley

ILLUSTRATIONS
Orrin Lundgren

SPECIAL PHOTOGRAPHY
Donald C. Noble

Library of Congress Cataloging-in-Publication Data

Noble, Carol R. (Carol Rasmussen), 1948-
　　Knitting Fair Isle mittens & gloves : 40 great-looking designs /
Carol Rasmussen Noble.— 1st ed.
　　　p. cm
　　Includes index.
　　ISBN 1-57990-253-7 (pbk.)
　　1. Knitting—Scotland—Fair Isle—Patterns. 2. Gloves—Scotland—Fair
Isle. 3. Mittens—Scotland—Fair Isle. I. Title: Knitting Fair Isle
mittens and gloves. II. Title
TT819 .N63 2002
746.43'20432—dc21　　　　　　　　　　　　　　　　2002066136

10 9 8 7 6 5 4 3 2 1

First Edition

Published by Lark Books, a division of
Sterling Publishing Co., Inc.
387 Park Avenue South, New York, N.Y, 10016

© 2002, Carol Rasmussen Noble

Distributed in Canada by Sterling Publishing,
c/o Canadian Manda Group, One Atlantic Ave., Suite 105
Toronto, Ontario, Canada M6K 3E7

Distributed in the U.K. by:
Guild of Master Craftsman Publications Ltd.
Castle Place, 166 High Street Lewes East Sussex, England BN7 1XU
Tel: (+ 44) 1273 477374 Fax: (+ 44) 1273 478606
Email: pubs@thegmcgroup.com, Web: www.gmcpublications.com

Distributed in Australia by Capricorn Link (Australia) Pty Ltd.,
P.O. Box 704, Windsor, NSW 2756 Australia

The written instructions, photographs, designs, patterns, and projects in
this volume are intended for the personal use of the reader and may be
reproduced for that purpose only. Any other use, especially commercial
use, is forbidden under law without written permission of the copyright
holder.

Every effort has been made to ensure that all the information in this book
is accurate. However, due to differing conditions, tools, and individual
skills, the publisher cannot be responsible for any injuries, losses, and
other damages that may result from the use of the information in this book.

If you have questions or comments about this book, please contact:
Lark Books
67 Broadway
Asheville, NC 28801
(828) 253-0467

Manufactured in China

ISBN 1-57990-253-7

TABLE OF CONTENTS

INTRODUCTION TO FAIR ISLE KNITTING 7

HISTORY OF KNITTING IN THE SHETLAND ISLES 8

KNITTING FAIR ISLE MITTENS & GLOVES TODAY 12

WOMEN'S FAIR ISLE MITTENS 18

Unst Flowers Variation 20

Fishermen's Mittens 22

Lerwick X's & O's 23

Diamonds Variation 24

Norwegian Stars in Naturals 26

Norwegian Stars in Blue 28

WOMEN'S FAIR ISLE FINGERLESS GLOVES 30

Snowflake 32

Celtic Knotwork 34

Tartan 36

Cross & Crown 37

Banded Christmas Star 38

Medallions in Aurora 40

Fingerless Fishermen's Gloves 42

BAIRNS' FAIR ISLE MITTS & GLOVES 44

X and Cross 46

Small Diamonds 47

Butterflies for Bairns 49

Peerie Hearts for Bairns 51

WOMEN'S FAIR ISLE GLOVES 52

Cunningsburgh Star 54

Cunningsburgh Star in Naturals with Hearts Gauntlets 56

Cuffed Cunningsburgh Star Variation 58

Cunningsburgh Star Outline Variation . . . 60

Traditional X's & O's 62

Traditional Allover 64

Earth-tones Allover Variation 66

Skuda in Red 68

Skuda in Greens 69

Traditional Star 70

Norwegian Star Variation 72

Whalsay Vertical Star 74

Confetti Star 76

Star Flower Variation 78

Open Medallions in Orange 80

Filled Medallions in Bright Colors 82

Ruby Wine Composite 84

Small Lozenge Star 86

Large Hearts 88

Butterflies 89

Wilma's 1928 Star 90

Forest Cross 92

Lace 94

ACKNOWLEDGMENTS 95

BIBLIOGRAPHY 96

INDEX 96

Introduction to
Fair Isle Knitting

Shetland is my special place, my refuge where, in confronting seas and storms and winds, I can savor the sweetness of being a survivor. In Shetland, you are never more than three miles from the rough seas. A gale in London is a fair breeze in Shetland. I love with a passion the bleak, rugged landscape—islands with precipitous cliffs full of nesting seabirds; hills covered by peat bogs, heather, and delicate wild flowers; dark inland lakes; and fingerlike voes from the encroaching sea. The climate—cold, rain, snow, ice, wind—appeals to me deeply on an atavistic level.

I would like to have visited Shetland in the early days of the century, before roads were paved and every-

Ruins of old stone croft houses are a familiar sight by the sea in Shetland. Stone, readily available from the fields that were cleared for pasture, was the only building material in this treeless, windswept land.

one had a car. I wonder if I could have survived the hard life and still created beauty with my knitting, humbly, like knitters of that time—in a stone, thatched-roof croft house, knitting long into the night by the spartan light of a peat fire. It was a life of poverty and hardship, but out of the harshness of such a life came an abundance of beauty in the work of those women's hands—knitting, produced as craft, not art, and yet an art form, steeped in tradition and vibrant with creativity.

Now, with North Sea oil money, the roads are paved and the people of Shetland have abandoned the old stone croft houses for modest, modern homes. But sheep are still everywhere, a primitive breed with fine and subtly colored soft wool especially good for knitting. No matter where you are in Shetland, you are reminded that these islands, since long before the Viking conquest, have been home to fishermen who also were farmers and sheepherders. Life has always been hard, and the people are frugal and self-effacing. I've been extremely fortunate in having good friends there.

Fair Isle is the term used to describe the style and technique of knitting that is particular to the Shetland Islands. Fair Isle is my favorite knitting technique. I love feeling part of the tradition, losing myself in the rhythm and balance of color, pattern and technique. Most Fair Isle knitting on Shetland is now done on small home knitting machines, but there are two items that still must be knit by hand (and this is the basis of my passion for them): lace, and the treasures in this book: the gloves and mittens (or mitts as the Shetlanders call them) made for women and children.

Native Shetland sheep graze in a verdant field along the rugged coastline of the northern coast of Unst, the northernmost of the Shetland Isles.

I began collecting gloves and mitts on my first trip to Shetland in 1995, at first out of necessity, having cold hands. Eventually my collection grew along with my fascination with what I would call these "small jewels" and I soon realized that each pair is highly individual, as individual as each knitter, even though all knitters work with a shared vocabulary.

I find the sheer exuberance of Shetland gloves to be overwhelming. As a textile collector and student, I've learned that when creativity within a certain tradition is combined with high technical skill, this doesn't mean there is a lack of innovation. On the contrary, such a combination becomes the cultural definition of innovation, as artisans redefine themselves with their shared vocabulary.

These pages contain much of the best of my collection, contemporary gloves and mitts from all over the islands, which represent the many branches of this tree of life that is traditional Shetland design. I hope that you will share my enthusiasm for these glorious textiles and find in them the joy that I do, whether you are a casual reader, a researcher, an expert, or a beginning knitter. This book is for all of you. Happy knitting!

History of Knitting
in the Shetland Isles

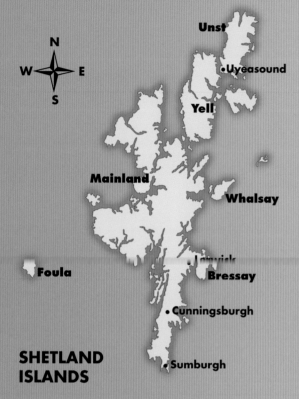

N W E S

Unst

•**Uyeasound**

Yell

Mainland

Whalsay

Foula

Lerwick

Bressay

•**Cunningsburgh**

SHETLAND ISLANDS

•**Sumburgh**

Fair Isle

S hetland is a group of small islands located about halfway between Scotland and Norway at the crossroads of the North Sea and the North Atlantic—at about the same latitude as Bergen, Norway. The northernmost island is Unst, and the southernmost, Fair Isle. The largest island is named Mainland.

The first settlers for which records exist were early Europeans that some historians have termed Albans. In the ninth century, King Harold Fairhair brought the islands under Norse control, and they remained so, changing hands between one Norse lord and another until, as part of an unpaid royal dowry, Shetland was annexed to Scotland in 1648.

After suffering under the misrule of notorious Scot earls such as Black Patie, who used forced labor to build his castle at Scalloway, Shetland became British territory by the Act of Union of 1707. Even today, however, Shetlanders don't consider themselves quite British, or even Scot, and maintain pride in their Norse heritage. They are Shetlanders first and foremost.

From about 1500, Shetland had healthy trading ties with the Baltics, Scandinavia, Germany, and Holland. It's probable that knitting came to Shetland at the same time as it was spreading

Muness Castle on the southeast corner of Unst, built in 1598, is the northernmost castle in Great Britain. In spite of its obscure location, the castle reflected the height of style and technology: a three story Z-plan of an oblong main block with diagonally opposed round towers. It was abandoned in 1750.

across the rest of Europe. During this period the Shetland hosiery trade—hosiery being an inclusive term that includes socks, mitts, gloves, nightcaps, and other similar garments—was born. Huge Dutch and German herring fleets fished Shetland's waters in the seventeenth century, trading their goods to the islanders for hosiery at large fairs in Bressay Sound on June 24 (St. John's Day), and at various trading stations set up in the hinterlands. Local women would bring a year's production of hosiery to trade for commercial goods they would not otherwise have access to.

Because knitwear is so perishable and few examples survive, it can only be assumed that this knitting was plain. The archeological find at the seventeenth-century burial site at Gunnister, however, shows both plain knitting on stockings, caps, and gloves; and rudimentary stranded color knitting on a small purse.

This period of prosperity for the knitters did not last. The French navy burned the Dutch fishing fleet in Shetland waters in 1702. This event, combined with a new tax on foreign salt, greatly depressed the herring trade in the eighteenth century. Shetland people became poorer and knitting in the islands declined in quality, even though at the same time, knitting was effectively becoming the currency of Shetland, used to pay rent and trade for commercial goods from local merchants.

So started the oppressive "truck system," in which women traded knitwear for goods and were at the mercy of the traders, a cruel reality that persisted until the end of World War II. The Industrial Revolution of the eighteenth century barely touched the Shetland hosiery trade; women knitted as individuals using wool from their own sheep to make trade goods along with clothing for themselves and their families. It wasn't until about 1835 to 1850 that the quality and design of Shetland knitting revived with the production of lace and new Fair Isle patterns, which subsequently have become so well known.

The term "Fair Isle" refers to the two-color per row stranded knitting done on all the islands, and is now the name used for the technique all over the world. How the term came into use is

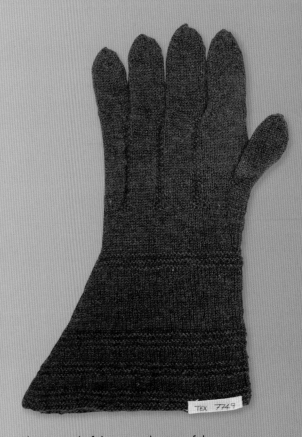

The original of this reproduction of the Gunnister glove, typical of a medieval gauntlet glove, is from the Gunnister site in Northmavine, Mainland. Coins dating from the seventeenth century were found in the pocket of an associated cote (tunic). The various pieces from the "Gunnister find" are the earliest known examples of Shetland knitting. *Courtesy of the Shetland Museum.*

This 50-year-old allover pattern glove in an unusual naturals color scheme really shows off the detail of the design. Courtesy of the Shetland Museum.

This reproduction of the earliest Fair Isle glove extant in Shetland was made in 1880. It was knitted on the island of Fair Isle. The original is in a private collection. Courtesy of the Shetland Museum.

somewhat of a mystery. The legend is that when they shipwrecked on Fair Isle in 1598, the Spanish sailors from the Armada's "El Gran Grifón," under command of the Duke of Medina, taught Fair Isle crofters to dye and knit colored patterns. It is a wonderful story, but there is no hard evidence that it's true.

More likely is that Fair Isle patterning grew out of trade with the Baltic countries, bringing in a flowering of new pattern ideas around 1800. From 1850 on, a wide variety of lace and both Fair Isle and plain knit items could be ordered from Shetland by catalogue. The earliest extant pieces of Fair Isle knitting from Fair Isle date from approximately 1880. By 1900, Fair Isle knitting was widespread on the Shetland Isles, and Shetland had given its name to the type of yarn used in the islands to this day to knit these garments. Fancy patterned gloves were the specialty of Whiteness and Wiesdale on Mainland.

Early gloves show allover random, but characteristic, Fair Isle patterning in the traditional red, yellow, brown, blue, and white. New influences like Sanquhar patterning (an overlay of boxes) and lace were readily absorbed and experimentation abounded in gloves, with geometrics being the dominant theme. As Fair Isle sweaters became fashionable, so did other Fair Isle items, including gloves.

Driving gloves with long gauntlets to cover the arms were popular in the early twentieth century. In this example, the gauntlets were meant to be folded back upon themselves. This is the boxy pattern called "Sanquhar" knitting, which at some early point traveled from Sanquhar, Scotland, to Shetland, probably with itinerant herring girls. Courtesy of the Shetland Museum.

In the early twentieth century, glove knitters were using all-over patterns with long, loose gauntlets (cuffs) that covered half the coat sleeve. Other items were being knit, for example, wrist warmers, and special thick half-finger mittens for fishermen. There was a greatly increased demand for gloves in 1937 and 1938 as the Depression eased. Gloves at that time featured two identical patterned bands going all around the hand with a neutral background, a style that is still being knit today.

Wristlets were worn in the nineteenth and early twentieth centuries for much the same reason as fingerless gloves are worn today— they provide warmth to the hand, while allowing the fingers to be free for work. Courtesy of the Shetland Museum.

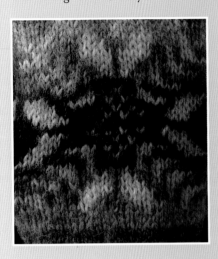

Shetland was the headquarters of the Norwegian resistance movement during World War II, which brought a large influx of Norwegian freedom fighters and refugees to the islands. With these people came the Norwegian star design, which proliferated into many variations when Shetland knitters enthusiastically took it up.

Some of the variations in style had gauntlets, patterned fingers, hems, and patterned thumbs. But the biggest change that these Norwegian-inspired gloves brought was the confinement of the star pattern to the back of the hand, with small geometrics on the palm. Norwegian stars are still popular in Fair Isle knitting today, but show their own Shetland flair in color and styling. Also dating from World War II is the overall star pattern unique to Shetland, which derives from the Norwegian Star design.

Even after the introduction of the home knitting machine in the 1950s, which revolutionized the industry, gloves and mitts continued to be made by hand. Also, at this time the tartan or argyle pattern was introduced from the Scottish mainland, which has further enriched the Fair Isle design palette.

GLOSSARY OF SHETLAND KNITTING TERMS

English	Shetland
bind off	cast off
cast on	lay up
child	bairn
cuff	gauntlet
first row or round	sweerie geng
glove	glāve
knitting	makkin
knitting belt	makkin belt
knitting needles	wires
knit two together	takk in or takk two together
little	peerie
mitten	mitt
row or round	geng
sweater	jumper
thumb	thoomb
wool	wirset
yarn over	cast up

Mittens & Gloves Today

Shetland yarn is known for its wonderful array of colors, and the sophistication with which these colors are combined.

Gloves are one of the few Shetland items that are still hand-knit today. Crofters send the fleece they don't sell to the Brora spinning mill in northern Scotland. When they receive back their yarn, it goes into the cupboard with the other bits and pieces of yarn until winter, when most knitting is done. Out of the natural fleece shades and odd lots of many leftover colors, a traditional glove is born. Color is a surprise, depending on what you have in your cupboard.

Knitting Fair Isle gloves and mittens is a cottage industry. It is still, and always has been, a way for women to make a little extra money. Shetland knitters don't see themselves as designers in the same sense that a knitter doing the same thing in the United States, Canada, or England might. Shetland knitters are craftspeople steeped in tradition and they recombine the elements of Fair Isle design in time-honored ways, making even the most modern or individualistic gloves traditional. Shetland knitters don't feel proprietary ownership of their designs; they emphasize that the designs belong to everyone. It is their common vocabulary.

It must be emphasized that these Fair Isle gloves are still trade goods. Gloves from the cupboard will go on consignment to one of the many small local knitwear businesses, appear at community center functions, or end up in a shop in Lerwick, the principal port and main tourist center. Some small entrepreneurs in more remote locations distribute yarn to a group of knitters who knit gloves that are then sold by the entrepreneur, usually in small shops.

Although there are a small number of mills in the world producing "Shetland style" wool, Shetlanders prefer their own home-grown wool, especially the wool manufactured and sold in Shetland by Jamieson & Smith. This Shetland wool is a specific weight and ply and is spun only from the fleece of Shetland breed sheep. Because Jamieson & Smith Shetland yarn comes in almost two hundred colors, it serves as a very exciting palette for knitters.

Color is at the heart of Shetland knitting, what makes it special. All the Shetland knitters I know have a sophisticated color sense and mix their shades, often ten or more, in a single glove, in an astonishingly beautiful and complex manner that non-Shetland knitters can only aspire to imitate. You can, of course, knit the mittens and gloves in any colors and any kind of wool you wish as long as it matches the gauge. However, if you want to knit a duplicate or near-duplicate of the Shetland gloves and mitts you see in the book, you'll probably want to use the Shetland knitters' favorite yarn. Color cards are available that have snippets of all the colors presently available. You can find this special yarn and the Fair Isle

The natural, undyed colors of Shetland fleece seem to capture the essence of the rugged island landscape. This is a sampling of these fleece colors.

A knitter from Unst demonstrates an antique Shetland knitting sheath, made of bird quills within a braided straw cover. The bird quills anchor the needle.

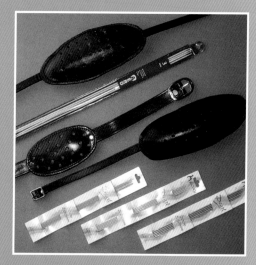

Unique to Shetland knitting is the use of long needles and knitting belts.

knitting needles and belts at selected stores, on the internet, and through mail order.

In order to provide you with the most up-to-date information, Lark Books has created a suppliers listing on its Web site, which is updated frequently. Visit the site at www.larkbooks.com, click on "Craft Supply Sources," and then click on the topic of Fair Isle knitting. You'll find numerous companies listed with their web address and/or mailing address and phone number.

Knitting the Shetland Way— on Long Needles with a Belt

The "Fair Isle" technique refers to knitting in the round with two colors per row. We use circular needles, typically in sizes 2.0 to 3.25 mm, depending on the item being knit. However, Shetland knitters still knit on 10-inch (10.6 cm) or 18-inch (45.7 cm) double-pointed needles, using a knitting belt—a technique that is a remnant of earlier knitting techniques that utilized a variety of needle lengths and, commonly, a curved knitting stick or sheath. This composite of English and Continental techniques was the

Here's the proper position of the belt, needles, and tie for Fair Isle knitting. Once you get familiar with it, it's quite easy.

norm in the eighteenth and nineteenth centuries in the hinterlands of England and Scotland. It can be used for projects of all sizes, from jumpers to gloves.

Shetland knitters use sets of four needles—three needles to hold the stitches and one, which we term the stationary needle, anchored in a hole in the knitting belt. The leather lozenge of the knitting belt is worn on the right front side, held in place by a leather belt that passes around the waist. Authentic Shetland knitting belts are stiff and sturdy, with horsehair or straw stuffing. Many are still made completely by hand.

Here's how to knit in the round on long double-pointed needles. Cast on the required number of stitches and divide them evenly onto the three needles. Although the cast-on varies from knitter to knitter, and also according to what is being knitted, a standard cable two-tailed cast-on is common. Place the beginning of the round in the middle of one needle to avoid loose stitches at the color changes.

On a large project such as a sweater (jumper), after a few inches have been knit, the knitter gathers up and secures the knitting to the belt with a triple length of yarn doubled over to make a slip-knot on the knitting. The other end is knotted and wrapped around or tucked into the left center side of the belt. The photo on the opposite page shows the proper position of the belt, needles and tie for knitting. Experienced Shetland knitters wrap the knot around a handkerchief and tuck it into the belt. A tie-up, although generally not needed for gloves and mittens, is very useful for larger projects.

Because you're knitting in Fair Isle technique, you'll have two working threads, each of a different color. In one form of the technique, you wrap the pattern color around your left index finger and the background color around your right index finger. Keep these fingers close to the knitting. To take a stitch, guide the stationary needle with your thumb and insert it into the first stitch knitwise.

Figure 1 shows the proper position of the yarn on the hands for the two-handed method.

Some knitters carry both threads on the right hand, with equal

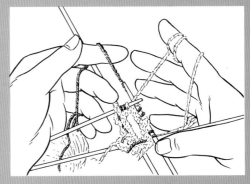

Fig. 1 How to position your hands and yarn when using the two-handed knitting method

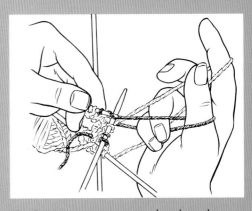

Fig. 2 How to position your hands and yarn when using the one-handed knitting method

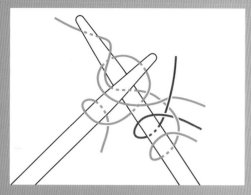

Fig. 3 How to position your yarns and needles when taking a pattern color stitch. Red indicates background color; green indicates pattern color.

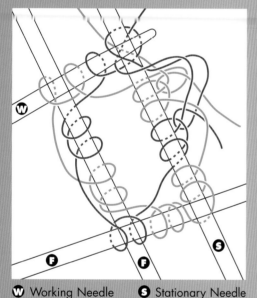

W Working Needle   **S** Stationary Needle
F Free Needle

Fig. 4 How to position your yarns and needles when taking a background stitch. Red is the background color; green is the pattern color. Notice how the red background color goes to the previous background color stitch on the previous row; the green pattern color goes to the previous pattern color stitch on the previous row.

results. Figure 2 shows the proper position of the yarn on the hands for this one-handed method.

Figure 3 is a diagram showing the positions of the needle and yarn while taking a pattern color stitch.

Figure 4 shows the correct position for making a background color stitch, and also illustrates the structure of the knitting on the needles in the Fair Isle two-color technique.

The basic idea is to knit on double-pointed needles in the round in the normal way, but with the stationary needle anchored in the knitting belt and free-standing so that you don't have to hold up the knitting or let go of it when taking a stitch. The technique works best if you sit up straight.

When a full needle has been knitted onto the stationary needle, remove this needle from the knitting belt. Loosen the slipknot holding the material already knitted and rearrange the knitting. Then place one point of the now-free needle, which is now the stationary needle, into the knitting belt and start again knitting from the second needle in the round.

For mittens and gloves, some knitters use long needles, but others use the 8-inch (20.3 cm) double-pointed needles which we are more familiar with, and which do not require a knitting belt. The technique is fundamentally the same.

Shaping the Gloves and Mittens

Hand wash the gloves and mittens after you've knit them, using cold water and baby shampoo. Don't wring out or agitate the knitting. Rinse well in cold water and wrap in a towel to gently squeeze out excess water. In Shetland, after they've been washed, the gloves and mittens are stretched on blocking boards to dry. These boards, with finger or mitten shapes, are mostly hand-made; often in the past, the wood came from shipwrecks. Thumb stretchers are either attached or separate. The mitten and glove boards in the photograph on the opposite page date from both the nineteenth and twentieth centuries. You can also block without boards by pinning the item into the appropriate shape and size on a rug or other base and allowing it to dry.

About the Sections in the Book

In the next sections are the individual projects, 40 of the most intriguing gloves and mittens from my collection. The categories are women's mittens, fingerless gloves, bairns' mitts and gloves, and women's gloves. Each section opens with basic instructions. All you have to do is plug in the patterns of your choice. If you wish, you can make the gloves just like the original, using the photos for color and pattern placement, or use your own color palette.

For each project there is a color photo showing the back and palm. The pattern bands for each are graphed in color, in sections of one repeat horizontally and vertically.

The bibliography lists the most important books on Fair Isle knitting that I used in my research and ones that will help you, if you wish, make a sweater or other garment using the classical techniques.

Happy knitting, or as they say in Shetland, happy makkin'!

Boards used for stretching washed mittens and gloves were handmade and passed down through a knitter's family.

Women's Fair Isle Mittens

Mittens for women in Shetland are a relatively new item of apparel. Traditionally, the women always wore gloves. It was during World War II that women's mittens were introduced into Shetland with the influx of Norwegian refugees. Norwegian people usually wear mittens with stars on them; gloves are less popular. Suddenly in Shetland, mitts became popular and have remained so.

Rather than making a mitten that really fits the hand well, Shetland knitters make them very long to accommodate their design preferences—they need more room on the mitts to include the double motif they're so fond of, for example, the three different star patterns we've included. With the double motif the knitters also pattern the area that connects the motifs, so there is a continuous pattern on the mitts.

To wear the mitts properly, you pull them down a ways on your arm, and they tend to flop a bit at your fingertips. Some of the patterns found on mitts today are a relatively new development. For example, the X's and O's pattern from the nineteenth century was traditionally found on sweaters. Today it's been sized down to make women's mitts as well.

BASIC WOMEN'S FAIR ISLE MITTENS

SIZE:
One size fits most.

FINISHED MEASUREMENT OF HAND:
Approximately 7 ½ inches (19 cm) in circumference and 7 ¾ inches (19.7 cm) from bottom of cuff to top of mitten

MATERIALS:
100% Shetland Wool. (1 ounce [56 g] = approximately 150 yards [137 m].) 1 ounce (56 g) Main Color and small quantities of Contrasting Colors for chosen Stitch Pattern.

NEEDLES:
Set of 5 double-pointed Size 1 (2.25-2.5 mm) *or size to obtain gauge.*

GAUGE:
32 stitches and 32 rounds = 4 inches (10 cm) using Size 1 needles in Fair Isle (stranded) knitting.
Take time to save time—check your gauge.

STITCH PATTERNS:
See Charts.
Note 1: Stitch Pattern repeats vary; it may be necessary to adjust total number of stitches after the cuff to fit the chosen Stitch Pattern; check number of stitches needed before increasing.
Note 2: When chosen Chart(s) have been completed, continue with Main Color only for remainder of mitten.

CUFF:
Using Main Color, cast on 56 stitches, distributed evenly on 4 needles. Total: 14 stitches on each needle. Place marker for beginning of round. Join, being careful not to twist stitches. Work in knit 1, purl 1 ribbing for 3 inches, increasing for chosen Stitch Pattern, on last round, if necessary.

HAND:
Change to Circular Stockinette Stitch (knit every round), and Fair Isle Stitch Pattern of choice; work even in pattern established until piece measures 2 ½ inches (6.4 cm) above cuff. **Thumb Opening, Right Mitten**: Continuing in pattern established, work across needles 1 and 2; from needle 3, knit 2, then knit 10 with waste yarn; return these 10 stitches to needle 3 and knit 10 in pattern, knit 2; work across needle 4 in pattern. **Thumb Opening, Left Mitten**: Continuing in pattern established, work across needle 1; from needle 2, knit 2, then knit 10 with waste yarn; return these 10 stitches to needle 2, and knit 10 in pattern, knit 2; work across needles 3 and 4 in pattern.

When piece measures approximately 4 inches (10 cm) above waste yarn for thumb, (approximately 6½ inches [16.5 cm] above cuff edge), begin shaping. (**Note**: Shaping will add approximately 1 ¼ inches (3.2 cm); adjust length if desired). * Work from needles 1 and 3 as: Knit 1; decrease one stitch by working a right slanting decrease (knit 2 together); knit to end. Work from needles 2 and 4 as: Knit to last 3 stitches; decrease one stitch by working a left slanting decrease (slip slip knit); knit 1. Repeat from * *every* round 9 times. Total 16 stitches (8 stitches for palm, and 8 for back of hand). Break yarn, leaving a 16-inch (41 cm) tail; using tapestry needle and tail, weave remaining stitches together.

THUMB:
Remove waste yarn; with Main Color (or color of choice), pick up 10 stitches from top and 10 stitches from bottom of thumb opening and distribute evenly on double-pointed needles; pick up 1 stitch at each corner. Total: 22 stitches. Work even until thumb measures 2 inches (5 cm) or ¼ inch (6.3 mm) less than desired length (thumb should reach to the middle of thumbnail before shaping). To shape thumb, work as for hand shaping, repeating from * 3 times. Break yarn, leaving a 12-inch (30.5 cm) tail; thread tail through remaining stitches, going through each stitch twice; gather stitches together and fasten off. Thumb measures approximately 2¼ inches (5.7 cm).

FINISHING:
Weave in ends neatly on reverse side. Steam block to even out stitches and obtain finished measurements.

Unst Flowers Variation

MAKER UNKNOWN

Shetlanders call these natural colors "fauns." The flower star pattern is typical of designs from Unst, and shows Shetland shading and palm patterning, with a plain thumb and ribbing.

After ribbing, work Rounds 1- 4 of Chart C around entire mitten; work Rounds 1-25, then Rounds 2-25 of Chart A on back of hand while working Chart B on palm in colors indicated; work Rounds 4 - 1 of Chart C around entire mitten; continue with Main Color for length.

CHART A Back of Hand

33 Stitch / 25 Round Repeat

KEY

☐ Main Color - Natural

■ Black

☐ White

▨ Taupe

▨ Brown

▨ Dark Brown

▨ Charcoal

▨ Grey

⊠ Chart B - use Contrasting Color used on back of mitten.

CHART B Palm

2 Stitch / 2 Round Repeat

CHART C Borders

4 Stitch / 4 Round Repeat

Fishermen's Mittens

MAKER UNKNOWN

CHART A
Back of Hand and Palm

6 Stitch / 4 Round Repeat

KEY

▨ Olive Green

☐ White

CHART B Thumb Gusset

Edge of Mitten

Palm

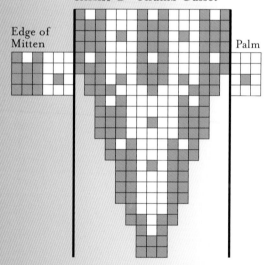

Ribbing: Work *4 rounds Olive, 4 rounds White; repeat from *twice, then work 4 rounds Olive. Begin Chart A with 5 White stripes/6 Olive stripes on back of mitten and 6 White/5 Dark on palm. Work thumb gusset as shown, inserting gusset in 2nd dark stripe on palm.

These fishermen's mittens from Yell are similar to Scandinavian fishermen's mittens, and have a long international history. This is a type of mitten Shetlanders knit for their own use, not for sale. They are meant for men, although this pair will fit a woman's hands. Usually these gloves were knit in black and white, so this color scheme is a bit unusual.

Lerwick X's & O's

MAKER UNKNOWN

The X's & O's pattern is the oldest Shetland knitting pattern, with roots in the mid-nineteenth century. From Lerwick, here's a mitten version in traditional colors. See the Traditional X's and O's glove pattern on page 62.

CHART A Back of Hand and Palm

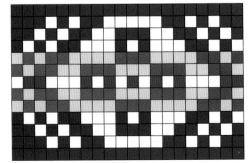

20 Stitch / 13 Round Repeat

KEY

■ Main Color - Dk. Blue
■ Dk. Red
□ White
■ Black
▨ Gold

CHART B
Borders

4 Stitch /
4 Round Repeat

Pattern is continuous around mitten. After ribbing, work Chart A, B, A, B, and A; then continue in Main Color for length.

CHART A Back of Hand

31 Stitch / 25 Round Repeat

KEY

■ Main Color - Grey

□ White

▨ Peach

▨ Gold

□ Yellow

⊠ Chart B - use Contrasting
    Color used on back of mitten.

CHART B Palm

4 Stitch / 4 Round Repeat

This pair of exuberant mittens from Unst is a hybrid. Its creative pattern has elements from both a star and a diamond combined in a single pattern.

After ribbing, work round 1 of Chart A around entire mitten; repeat rounds 2-25 of Chart A twice on back of mitten while working Chart B on palm, in colors indicated; continue with Main Color for length. Work thumb with Main Color.

Norwegian Stars in Naturals

MAKER UNKNOWN

This pair of Unst mittens shows the traditional double pattern on the back with a Shetland geometric shaded palm. It has a predominately natural fauns color scheme but with high contrasts.

CHART A Back of Hand

33 Stitch / 25 Round Repeat

After ribbing, work rounds 1-6 of Chart C around entire mitten; work rounds 1-25, then 2-25 of Chart A on back of mitten while working Chart B on palm in colors indicated, (begin round 1 of Chart B, repeat rounds 2 and 3 for length, end round 4); work rounds 6-1 of Chart C around entire mitten, then continue with Main Color for length.

KEY

▨ Main Color - Beige Heather

■ Brown

□ White

▨ Grey

■ Dk. Brown

▨ Beige

⊠ Chart B - use Contrasting Color used on back of mitten.

⊡ Chart B - use Background Color used on back of mitten.

CHART B Palm

End
Repeat
Begin

6 Stitch / 2 Round Repeat

CHART C
Borders

2 Stitch /
6 Round Repeat

CHART A Back of Hand

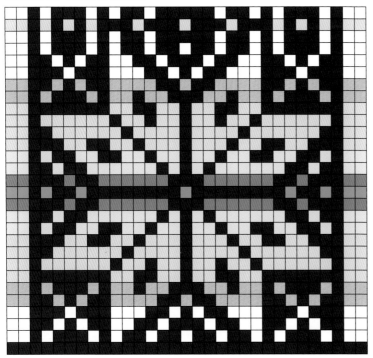

31 Stitch / 29 Round Repeat

Norwegian Stars in Blue

KNIT BY
KATHLEEN SMITH

This is a classic Shetland Norwegian Star mitten, with Shetland shading and a Shetland palm. Shetland mittens tend to be quite long, flopping over a bit at the fingertips, such as this pair.

After ribbing, work round 1 of Chart A around entire mitten; repeat rounds 2-29 of Chart A twice on back of mitten while working Chart B on palm, using colors indicated, for length. Work thumb same as palm.

KEY

- ■ Main Color - Navy
- □ White
- ▨ Silver
- ▨ Blue Heather
- ▨ Medium Blue
- □ Lt. Blue
- ▨ Green
- ⊠ Chart B - use Contrasting Color used on back of mitten.

CHART B Palm and Thumb

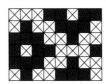

8 Stitch / 6 Round Repeat

Women's Fair Isle Fingerless Gloves

Traditionally both men and women wore fingerless gloves. They were ideally suited to people who used their hands in their work. Homes in Shetland didn't have any central heating, just warmth from the hearth, so wintertime was often bitter cold, even indoors. The women wore fingerless gloves so they could continue to knit despite the cold. Fishermen wore fingerless gloves on the fishing boats to keep their fingers free for removing fish-hooks. Nowadays on Shetland, only women wear fingerless gloves, not the men. But they are growing in popularity among teenagers, who enjoy the warmth the glove offers while allowing dexterity of the fingers. Another reason for the fingerless glove's popularity is that it is much easier to knit than a glove with fingers. You don't have to worry too much about the fit of the glove and it takes a lot less time to complete.

BASIC WOMEN'S FAIR ISLE FINGERLESS GLOVES

SIZE:
One size fits most.

FINISHED MEASUREMENT:
Approximately 7 inches (17.8 cm) in circumference and 4½ inches (11.4 cm) from top of cuff to beginning of finger join.

MATERIALS:
100% Shetland Wool. (1 ounce [56 g] = approximately 150 yards [137 m]). 1 ounce (56 g) Main Color and small quantities of Contrasting Colors for chosen Stitch Pattern.

NEEDLES:
Set of 5 double-pointed needles Size 0 (2mm) *or size to obtain gauge.*

GAUGE:
36 stitches and 36 rounds = 4 inches (10 cm) using Size 0 needles in Fair Isle (stranded) knitting. *Take time to save time—check your gauge.*

STITCH PATTERNS:
See Charts.

Note 1: Stitch Pattern repeats vary. It may be necessary to adjust total number of stitches after the cuff to fit the chosen Stitch Pattern; check number of stitches needed before increasing.

Note 2: When chosen Chart(s) have been completed, continue with Main Color (or color of choice) for remainder of glove.

CUFF:
Using Main Color, cast on 54 stitches, distributed evenly on 4 needles; place marker for beginning of round. Join, being careful not to twist stitches. Work in knit 1, purl 1 ribbing for 2¾ inches (7 cm), increasing 8 stitches (or number for chosen Stitch pattern) evenly on last round. Total: 62 stitches (needles 1 and 3: 15 stitches; needles 2 and 4: 16 stitches).

HAND:
Change to Circular Stockinette stitch (knit every round), and Fair Isle Stitch Pattern of choice; work even in pattern established until piece measures 2 ½ inches (6.4 cm) above cuff. **Thumb Opening, Right**

Glove: Continuing in pattern established, work across needles 1 and 2; from needle 3, knit 2; then knit 10 with waste yarn; return these 10 stitches to needle 3, and knit 10 in pattern; knit 3; work across needle 4 in pattern. **Thumb Opening, Left Glove:** Continuing in pattern established, work across needle 1; from needle 2, knit 4; then knit 10 with waste yarn; return these 10 stitches to needle 2 and knit 10 in pattern; knit 2; work across needles 3 and 4 in pattern.

When piece measures 2 inches (5 cm) from waste yarn for thumb, (approximately 4½ inches [11.4 cm] above cuff), place all stitches on a circular stitch holder or waste yarn, keeping marker for beginning of round in place to separate back of hand from palm.

JOIN EDGE/FINGER SECTIONS:
Work knit 1, purl 1 ribbing for ½ (1.3 cm) to 1 inch (2.5 cm) to create finger sections as follows:
Little finger: With Main Color (or color of choice), pick up from holder and place on double pointed needles 7 stitches from back of hand and 7 stitches from palm. Total: 14 stitches. Work knit 1, purl 1 ribbing to desired length; bind off loosely in pattern. **Ring, Middle and Index Fingers**: Working one finger at a time, pick up 8 stitches from back of hand and 8 stitches from palm for each finger. Work as for little finger.

THUMB:
Remove waste yarn; with Main Color (or color of choice), pick up and place on double-pointed needles 10 stitches from top and 10 stitches from bottom of opening and distribute evenly on double-pointed needles; pick up one stitch at each corner. Total: 22 stitches. Work knit 1, purl 1 ribbing to desired length; bind off loosely in pattern.

FINISHING:
Weave in ends neatly on reverse side. Steam block to even out stitches and obtain finished measurements.

CHART A Back of Hand

31 Stitch / 25 Round Repeat

After working ribbing, work Chart D once around entire glove;
work Chart A on back of hand while working Chart B on palm;
work Chart C around entire glove.

KEY

■ Main Color - Dk. Grey

☐ White

▨ Silver

⊠ Chart B - work with
Contrasting Color
used on back of glove.

CHART B Palm

4 Stitch / 4 Round Repeat

CHART C Top Border

2 Stitch / 4 Round Repeat

CHART D Bottom Border

2 Stitch / 4 Round Repeat

Snowflake

MAKER UNKNOWN

These fingerless gloves from Lerwick are highly unusual. The snowflake pattern is elongated, and the palm has a unique design. In addition, the all-natural grey shading with white is quite subtle and muted.

Celtic Knotwork

KNIT BY BARBARA ISBISTER

Shetland had no Celtic settlements, so the Celtic knot isn't a traditional Shetland motif. And yet, even with an asymmetrical format, the design of these gloves has transformed the Celtic knot into a very typical Shetland fingerless glove, in a traditional natural color scheme.

CHART A Pattern Band #1

8 Stitch / 12 Round Repeat

KEY

Brown – Main Color

Black

Beige

Taupe

Grey

CHART B Pattern Band #2

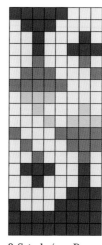

8 Stitch / 19 Round Repeat

Pattern is continuous around glove. After ribbing, work Chart A, then Chart B; work remainder of glove with Main Color.

Tartan

MAKER UNKNOWN

CHART A
Back of Hand and Palm

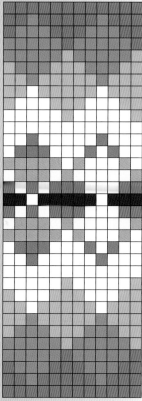

12 Stitch / 33 Round Repeat

KEY

- ☐ White
- ☐ Pale Yellow
- ☐ Grey-Green
- ☐ Purple-Red
- ☐ Purple Heather
- ☐ Maroon
- ☐ Lilac
- ☐ Loden green

Work Chart A around entire glove.

Although done up in bright colors, these fingerless gloves from Lerwick have a dainty, conservative look. The pattern of interlocking diamonds was developed in the 1950s on Shetland. It can now be found on a variety of garments, but its home remains the fingerless glove.

Cross & Crown

MAKER UNKNOWN

This is the first pair of gloves I bought in Shetland, at the Old Haa Museum on the Island of Yell. It was 1995, the weather was miserable, my hands were terribly cold, and these gloves were a godsend. I didn't know it at the time, but it turns out all the patterns and colors are traditional.

CHART A Back of Hand and Palm

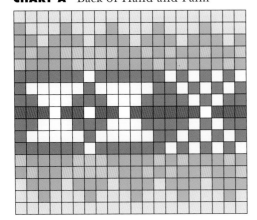

20 Stitch / 17 Round Repeat

KEY

- ☐ White
- ▨ Turquoise
- ☐ Pale Yellow
- ▨ Yellow Orange
- ▨ Brown
- ▨ Dk. Red
- ▨ Dk. Brown
- ☐ Beige

CHART B Border

4 Stitch / 6 Round Repeat

After ribbing, work Chart A, then Chart B, then Chart A around entire glove.

CHART A Back of Hand

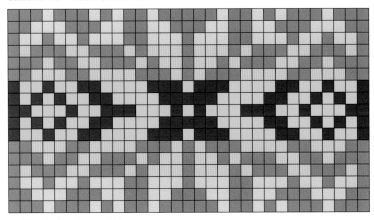

31 Stitch / 17 Round Repeat

KEY

▨	Dk. Loden Green - Main Color
▨	Dk. Brown
▨	Red
▨	Silver Grey
▨	Gold
▨	Yellow Green
⊠	Chart B - Use Contrasting Color used on back of glove.
⊡	Chart B- use Background Color used on back of glove.

After working ribbing, work Chart C around entire glove. Work Chart A on back of glove while working Chart B on palm in colors indicated; repeat Chart C around entire glove; work remainder of glove in Main Color.

CHART B Palm

2 Stitch / 2 Round Repeat

CHART C Borders

6 Stitch / 10 Round Repeat

Banded Christmas Star

DESIGNED BY
WILMA MALCOLMSON

This is a typical design by Wilma Malcolmson, with one pattern band on the back only and the other pattern going around the glove. More colorful than many of Wilma's gloves, it reminds me of Christmas, so that's what I named it.

Medallions in Aurora

DESIGNED BY
WILMA MALCOLMSON

Heathers abound in the unusual low-contrast color scheme of these fingerless gloves. Designer Wilma Malcolmson of Cunningsburgh, Mainland, often uses colors much closer in shade than ordinarily found in a typical Shetland glove. For very different versions of the medallion pattern see two projects for full-fingered women's gloves, Open Medallions in Orange on page 80 and Filled Medallions in Bright Colors on page 82.

CHART A Back of Hand

35 Stitch / 17 Round Repeat

KEY

- ☐ *Maroon - background
- ■ Magenta
- ▨ Yellow-Orange
- ▨ Red-Orange
- ▨ Turquoise

*Background Maroon color shown as White for clarity.

CHART B Palm

4 Stitch / 4 Round Repeat

- ☐ *Maroon
- ■ Contrasting Color

Work Chart D around glove; then work Chart B on palm, while working Chart A on back of hand; work Chart C around glove.

CHART C Top Border

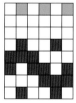

6 Stitch / 8 Round Repeat

CHART D Bottom Border

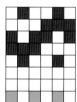

6 Stitch / 8 Round Repeat

CHART A Back of Hand

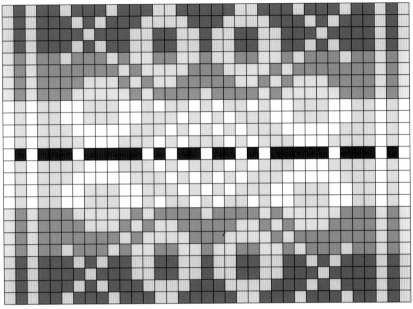

35 Stitch / 25 Round Repeat

After working ribbing, work rounds 1-5 of Chart C around entire glove; work Chart A on back of glove while working Chart B on palm in colors indicated; work rounds 5-1 of Chart C around entire glove; work remainder of glove in Main Color.

KEY

■ Dk. Brown - Main Color

▨ Salmon

■ Blue

☐ Yellow

▨ Sky Blue

☐ Pale Blue

☐ White

■ Navy Blue

⊠ Chart B - Use Contrasting Color used on back of glove.

⊡ Chart B- use Background Color used on back of glove.

Fingerless Fishermen's Gloves

MAKER UNKNOWN

These gloves from Unst show a highly creative pattern in a traditional style. Although this pair is sized for a woman's hands, such gloves used to be made only for men working on fishing boats. The extra-long fingers were fashioned so that the men's fingertips were free to remove fishhooks.

CHART B Palm

6 Stitch / 2 Round Repeat

CHART C
Borders

2 Stitch /
5 Round Repeat

Bairns' Fair Isle Gloves & Mitts

Unlike gloves and mitts for adults, those for children are bright and cheerful. Toddlers, about age two to three years, wear mitts with two bands of color. The older children of school age wear larger mitts, with three bands of color.

It's very unusual to find bairns' gloves, such as the pair in this section, because children in Shetland usually wear mittens. Mitts, of course, are easier to knit, and more practical than gloves since kids outgrow them quickly.

My friend, knitter Margaret Peterson of Unst, obtained the projects in this section for me. Alas, the makers are unknown.

BASIC CHILDREN'S FAIR ISLE MITTENS

SIZE:
One size fits most.

FINISHED MEASUREMENT OF HAND:
Approximately 7 ½ inches (19 cm) in circumference and 6 inches (15.2 cm) long.

MATERIALS:
100% Shetland Wool. (1 ounce [56 g] = approximately 150 yards [137 m].) 1 ounce (56 g) Main Color and small quantities of Contrasting Colors for chosen Stitch Pattern.

NEEDLES:
Set of 5 double-pointed Size 0 (2 mm) *or size to obtain gauge.*

GAUGE:
36 stitches and 36 rounds = 4 inches (10 cm) using Size 0 needles in Fair Isle (stranded) knitting.
Take time to save time—check your gauge.

STITCH PATTERNS:
See Charts.

Note 1: Stitch Pattern repeats vary. It may be necessary to adjust total number of stitches after the cuff to fit the chosen Stitch Pattern; check number of stitches needed before increasing.

Note 2: When chosen Chart(s) have been completed, continue with Main Color only for remainder of mitten.

CUFF:
Using Main Color, cast on 50 stitches, distributed as follows: needles 1 and 3: 12 stitches; needles 2 and 4: 13 stitches. Place marker for beginning of round. Join, being careful not to twist stitches. Work in knit 1, purl 1 ribbing for 2 ¼ inches (5.7 cm), increasing 10 stitches (or number for chosen Stitch Pattern), evenly on last round. Total: 60 stitches, 15 on each needle.

HAND:
Change to Circular Stockinette stitch (knit every round), and Fair Isle Stitch Pattern of choice; work even in pattern established until piece measures 1 ¾ inches (4.4 cm) above cuff. **Thumb Opening, Right Mitten:** Continuing in pattern established, work across needles 1 and 2; from needle 3, knit 9 with waste yarn; return these 9 stitches to needle 3, and knit 9 in pattern; knit 6; work across needle 4 in pattern. **Thumb Opening, Left Mitten:** Continue in pattern established, work across needle 1; from needle 2, knit 6; then knit 9 with waste yarn, return these 9 stitches to needle 2, and knit 9 in pattern; work across needles 3 and 4 in pattern established.

When piece measures 3 inches (7.6 cm) above waste yarn for thumb, (approximately 4 ¾ inches [12.1 cm] above cuff edge), begin shaping. Shaping will add approximately 1 ¼ inches (3.2 cm); adjust length if desired. *Work from needles 1 and 3 as: Knit 1; decrease one stitch by working a right slanting decrease (knit 2 together); knit to end. Work from needles 2 and 4 as: Knit to last 3 stitches; decrease one stitch by working a left slanting decrease (slip slip knit); knit 1. Repeat from *every* round 10 times. Total: 16 stitches (8 stitches for palm, and 8 for back of hand). Break yarn, leaving a 16-inch (40.6 cm) tail; using tapestry needle and tail, weave remaining stitches together.

THUMB:
Remove waste yarn; with Main Color (or color of choice), pick up 9 stitches from top and 9 stitches from bottom of thumb opening, and distribute evenly on double-pointed needles; pick up one stitch at each corner. Total: 20 stitches for thumb. Work even until thumb measures 2 inches (5 cm) or ¼ inch (6.35 mm) less than desired length. Thumb should reach middle of thumbnail before shaping. To shape thumb, (Knit 2 together around) twice. Total: 5 stitches remaining. Break yarn, leaving a 12-inch (30.5 cm) tail; thread tail through remaining stitches, going through each stitch twice; gather stitches together and fasten off. Thumb measures approximately 2 ¼ inches (5.7 cm).

FINISHING:
Weave in ends neatly on reverse side. Steam block to even out stitches and obtain finished measurements.

X and Cross

MAKER UNKNOWN

I have never seen anything even similar to this pair of children's mitts from Unst. It is probably a rare and very old pattern. Like all mitts for older children, this one has three pattern bands.

KEY

- ☐ Main Color
- ▨ Blue
- ▨ Medium Brown
- ☐ Pale Yellow
- ☐ White
- ▨ Cranberry
- ■ Black

CHART A Back of Hand and Palm

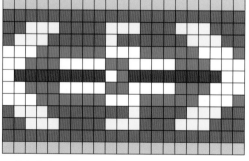

21 Stitch / 13 Round Repeat

CHART B
Top and Bottom Borders

6 Stitch / 6 Round Repeat

CHART C Middle Borders

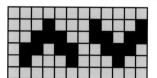

12 Stitch / 6 Round Repeat

Stripe Sequence: Work Chart B, Chart A, Chart C, Chart A; work Chart B using Medium Brown as Contrasting Color; then repeat Chart A.

MAKER UNKNOWN

F or a child's mitten, this color
scheme is subdued. This pattern
is a hybrid of diamonds, deriving from
the old X's & O's pattern of two centuries
ago. (See the women's glove version on
page 62.)

CHART A Back of Hand and Palm

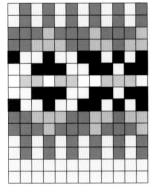

12 Stitch / 15 Round Repeat
Work Chart A 3 times.

KEY

☐ Main Color

▨ Mahogany

▨ Peach

■ Black

☐ Lt. Yellow

☐ White

▨ Grey

Small Diamonds

BASIC TODDLER'S FAIR ISLE MITTENS

SIZE:
One size fits most.

FINISHED MEASUREMENT OF HAND:
Approximately 5 inches (12.7 cm) in circumference and 4½ inches (11.4 cm) long.

MATERIALS:
100% Shetland Wool. (1 ounce [56 g] = approximately 150 yards [137 m].) 1 ounce (56 g) Main Color and small quantities of Contrasting Colors for chosen Stitch Pattern.

NEEDLES:
Set of 5 double-pointed Size 0 (2 mm) *or size to obtain gauge.*

GAUGE:
36 stitches and 36 rounds = 4 inches (10 cm) using Size 0 needles in Fair Isle (stranded) knitting. *Take time to save time—check your gauge.*

STITCH PATTERNS:
See Charts.
Note 1: Stitch Pattern repeats vary. It may be necessary to adjust total number of stitches after the cuff to fit the chosen Stitch Pattern; check number of stitches needed before increasing.
Note 2: When chosen Chart(s) have been completed, continue with Main Color only for remainder of mitten.

CUFF:
Using Main Color, cast on 52 stitches, distributed evenly on 4 needles. Total: 13 stitches on each needle. Place marker for beginning of round. Join, being careful not to twist stitches. Work in knit 2, purl 2 ribbing for 2¼ inches (5.7 cm), increasing for chosen Stitch Pattern on last round, if necessary.

HAND:
Change to Circular Stockinette Stitch (knit every round), and Fair Isle Stitch. Work even in pattern established until piece measures 1¾ inches (6.4 cm) above cuff. **Thumb Opening, Right Mitten:** Continuing in pattern established, work across nee-

dles 1 and 2; from needle 3, knit 8 with waste yarn; return these 8 stitches to needle 3 and knit 8 in pattern; knit 5; work across needle 4 in pattern.
Thumb Opening, Left Mitten: Continuing in pattern established, work across needle 1; from needle 2, knit 5; then knit 8 with waste yarn; return these 8 stitches to needle 2 and knit 8 in pattern; work across needles 3 and 4 in pattern.

When piece measures 1¾ inches (6.4 cm) from waste yarn for thumb (approximately 3½ inches [8/9 cm] above cuff edge), begin shaping. Shaping will add approximately 1¼ inches (3.2 cm), adjust length if desired. * Work from needles 1 and 3 as: Knit 1; decrease one stitch by working a right slanting decrease (knit 2 together); knit to end. Work from needles 2 and 4 as: Knit to last 3 stitches; decrease one stitch by working a left slanting decrease (slip slip knit); knit 1. Repeat from * *every* round 9 times. Total: 12 stitches (6 stitches for palm, and 6 for back of hand). Break yarn, leaving a 16-inch (40.6 cm) tail; using tapestry needle and tail, weave remaining stitches together.

THUMB:
Remove waste yarn; using Main Color (or color of choice), pick up 8 stitches from top and 8 stitches from bottom of thumb opening and distribute evenly on double pointed needles; pick up 1 stitch at each corner. Total: 18 stitches for thumb. Work even until thumb measures 1¼ inches (3.2 cm) or ¼ inch (6.35 mm) less than desired length. Thumb should reach middle of thumbnail before shaping. To shape thumb: Knit 2 together around twice. Break yarn, leaving a 12-inch (30.5 cm) tail; thread tail through remaining stitches, going through each stitch twice; gather stitches together and fasten off. Thumb measures approximately 1½ inches (3.8 cm).

FINISHING:
Weave in ends neatly on reverse side. Steam block to even out stitches and obtain finished measurements.

Butterflies for Bairns

MAKER UNKNOWN

This eye-dazzling mitten from Unst has a butterfly pattern that just seems to want to fly away. Bairns' mittens typically have very bright colors. (See the women's glove version on page 89.)

CHART A Back of Hand and Palm

12 Stitch / 15 Round Repeat

CHART B
Border

2 Stitch /
4 Round Repeat

KEY

- ■ Main Color-Red
- ▦ Aqua
- □ White
- ▨ Jade Green
- ▤ Pale Dull Yellow
- ▥ Peach
- ▨ Brown
- □ Butter Yellow

Stripe sequence:
Work 15 rounds
Chart A;
4 rounds Chart B;
15 rounds Chart A.

BASIC TODDLER'S FAIR ISLE GLOVES

SIZE:
One size fits most.

FINISHED MEASUREMENTS:
Approximately 5 ¼ inches (13.3 cm) in circumference and 3 inches (7.6 cm) long from cuff to beginning of fingers.

MATERIALS:
100% Shetland Wool. (1 ounce [56 g] = approximately 150 yards [137 m].) 1 ounce (56 g) Main Color and small quantities of Contrasting Colors for chosen Stitch Pattern.

NEEDLES:
Set of 5 double pointed Size 0 (2 mm) *or size to obtain gauge.*

GAUGE:
36 stitches and 36 rounds = 4 inches (10 cm) using Size 0 needles in Fair Isle (stranded) knitting.
Take time to save time—check your gauge.

STITCH PATTERNS:
See Charts.
Note 1: Stitch pattern repeats vary; it may be necessary to adjust total number of stitches after the cuff to fit the chosen Stitch Pattern; check number of stitches needed before increasing.
Note 2: When chosen Chart(s) have been completed, continue with Main Color (or color of choice) for remainder of glove.

CUFF:
Using Main Color, cast on 36 stitches, distributed evenly on 4 needles; place marker for beginning of round. Join, being careful not to twist stitches. Work in knit 1, purl 1 ribbing for 1 ¾ inches (4.4 cm), increasing 12 stitches (or number for chosen Stitch Pattern), evenly on last round. Total: 48 stitches, 12 on each needle.

HAND:
Change to Circular Stockinette Stitch (knit every round) and Fair Isle Stitch Pattern of choice. Work even in pattern established until piece measures 1 ½ inches (3.8 cm) above cuff. **Thumb Opening, Right Glove**: Continuing in pattern established, work across needles 1 and 2; from needle 3, knit 8 with waste yarn; return these 8 stitches to needle 3; knit 8 in pattern; knit 4; work across needle 4 in pattern. **Thumb Opening, Left Glove**: Continuing in pattern

established, work across needle 1; from needle 2, knit 4; then knit 8 with waste yarn; return these 8 stitches to needle 2 and knit 8 in pattern; work across needles 3 and 4 in pattern.

When piece measures 1 ½ inches (3.8 cm) from waste yarn for thumb (approximately 3 inches [7.6 cm] above cuff edge), place all stitches on a circular stitch holder or waste yarn, keeping marker for beginning of round in place to separate back of hand from palm.

FINGERS:
Little finger: With Main Color (or color of choice), pick up from holder and place on double-pointed needles 6 stitches from back of hand, and 6 stitches from palm. Increase one stitch on inside of finger to join. Total: 13 stitches. Work even until little finger measures 1 ¼ inches (3.2 cm) or ¼ inch (6.3 mm) less than desired length. Finger should reach middle of fingernail before shaping. To shape fingertip: (Knit 2 together around) twice. Break yarn, leaving a 12-inch (30.5 cm) tail; thread tail through remaining stitches, going through each stitch twice; gather stitches together and fasten off. Little finger measures approximately 1 ½ inches (3.8 cm).
Ring finger: Working as for little finger, pick up next 6 stitches from back of hand and 6 stitches from palm. Increase one stitch at inside of finger and pick up one stitch between ring finger and little finger. Total: 14 stitches. Work as for little finger until finger measures 1 ¾ inches (4.4 cm) or ¼ inch (6.3 mm) less than desired length. Finger should reach middle of fingernail before shaping. Shape fingertip as for little finger. Finger measures approximately 2 inches (5 cm).
Middle and Index fingers: Work as for ring finger, omitting increase at outside of index finger.

THUMB:
Remove waste yarn; with Main Color (or color of choice), pick up 8 stitches from top and 8 stitches from bottom of opening and distribute evenly on double-pointed needles; pick up one stitch at each corner. Total: 18 stitches for thumb. Work even until thumb measures 1 ¼ inches (3.2 cm) or ¼ inch (6.3 mm) less than desired length. Shape as for fingers. Thumb measures approximately 1 ½ inches (3.8 cm).

FINISHING:
Weave in ends neatly on reverse side. Steam block to even out stitches and obtain finished measurements.

Peerie Hearts for Bairns

MAKER UNKNOWN

This charming peerie glove for bairns from Unst has a color scheme that literally brings it to life on a toddler's hands. (See the women's glove variation of this pattern on page 88.)

KEY

- ☐ Main Color
- ☐ Beige
- ▨ Aqua
- ▨ Tangerine
- ☐ Peach
- ☐ Pale Yellow
- ▨ Brown

CHART A Back of Hand and Palm

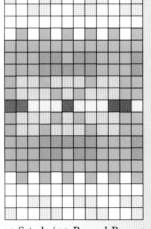

Work 12 stitch/19 round repeat around glove once.

12 Stitch / 19 Round Repeat

Women's Fair Isle Gloves

omen's gloves have been knit in Shetland since the sixteenth century, and patterned gloves dating from the mid-nineteenth century are known. In the Shetland Museum in Lerwick are displayed mail-order catalogues produced from about 1850 to 1880, depicting Shetland items that could by ordered custom-knit. These catalogues were prepared by merchants in Lerwick and sent to England. Women on Shetland traditionally wore gloves instead of mittens, and this is still true today. Men's gloves are rarer and are almost never patterned.

Shetland gloves have evolved over time in both style and pattern, but can readily be distinguished from gloves originating in other North Sea countries. Some influences have been made by Norwegian gloves and mittens brought to Shetland during World War II. The zig-zag lace glove seems to have Icelandic antecedents, although in Iceland they are always made in naturals and in Shetland, always in color. Unique to Shetland is the glove pattern referred to as "allover." It may have some indirect relation to the Norwegian Star. However, in its present form, which has been knit for at least 50 years, allovers are unique to Shetland and have no relatives in North Sea or Baltic countries.

BASIC WOMEN'S FAIR ISLE GLOVES

SIZE:
One size fits most.

FINISHED MEASUREMENTS:
Approximately 7 ½ inches (17.8 cm) in circumference and 4 ¼ inches (10.8 cm) long from top of cuff to beginning of fingers.

MATERIALS:
100% Shetland Wool. (1 ounce [56 g] = approximately 150 yards [137 m]). 1 ounce (56 g) Main Color and small quantities of Contrasting Colors for chosen Stitch Pattern.

NEEDLES:
Set of 5 double-pointed Size 1 (2.25 to 2.5 mm) *or size to obtain gauge*.

GAUGE:

32 stitches and 32 rounds = 4 inches (10 cm) using Size I needles in Fair Isle (stranded) knitting. *Take time to save time—check your gauge.*

STITCH PATTERNS:

See Charts.

Note 1: Stitch pattern repeats vary; it may be necessary to adjust total number of stitches after the cuff to fit the chosen Stitch Pattern; check number of stitches needed before increasing.

Note 2: When chosen Chart(s) have been completed, continue with Main Color (or color of choice) for remainder of glove.

CUFF:

Using Main Color, cast on 42 stitches distributed evenly on 4 needles; place marker for beginning of round. Join, being careful not to twist stitches. Work in knit I, purl I rib for 3 inches (7.6 cm), increasing 18 stitches (or number for chosen stitch pattern) evenly on last round. Total: 60 stitches, 15 on each needle.

HAND:

Change to Circular Stockinette Stitch (knit every round) and Fair Isle Stitch Pattern of choice; work even in pattern established until piece measures 2⅛ inches (5.4 cm) above cuff. **Thumb Opening, Right Glove:** Continue in pattern established, work across needles I and 2; from needle 3, knit 9 with waste yarn; return these 9 stitches to needle 3 and knit 9 in pattern established; knit 6 in pattern established; work across needle 4 in pattern established. **Thumb Opening, Left Glove:** Continue in pattern established, work across needle I; from needle 2, knit 6 in pattern established; knit 9 with waste yarn, return these 9 stitches to needle 2, and knit 9 in pattern established; work across needles 3 and 4 in pattern established.

When piece measures 2⅛ inches (5.4 cm) from waste yarn for thumb, (approximately 4¼ inches [10.8 cm] above cuff edge), place all stitches on a circular stitch holder or waste yarn, keeping marker for beginning of round in place to separate back of glove from palm.

FINGERS:

Little finger: With Main Color (or color of choice), pick up from holder and place on double-pointed needles 8 stitches from back of glove, and 8 stitches from palm; on inside of finger, cast on 2 stitches. Total: 18 stitches. Work even until finger measures 1¾ inches (4.4 cm) or ¼ inch (6.3 mm) less than desired length. Finger should reach middle of nail of little finger before shaping. To shape fingertip: for decrease round, on each needle knit 2 together, work to last 2 stitches, slip slip knit. Total: 8 stitches decreased. Work I round even. Repeat decrease round once; break yarn, leaving a 12-inch tail (30.5 cm); thread tail through remaining stitches, going through each stitch twice; gather stitches together and fasten off. The little finger measures approximately 2 inches (5 cm).

Ring and Middle Finger: With Main Color (or color of choice), pick up from holder and place on double-pointed needles 7 stitches from back of glove, and 7 stitches from palm; pick up 2 stitches from cast-on stitches of previous finger and cast on 2 stitches at opposite side. Total: 18 stitches distributed evenly on 4 needles. Work as for little finger to the middle of nail; shape fingertip as for little finger. Ring finger measures approximately 2¾ inches (6.9 cm); middle finger measures approximately 3¼ inches (8.3 cm).

Index Finger: With Main Color (or color of choice), pick up from holder and place on double-pointed needles 8 stitches from back of glove, and 8 stitches from palm; on inside of finger, pick up 2 stitches from cast-on stitches of previous finger. Total: 18 stitches distributed evenly on 4 needles. Work as for little finger to the middle of nail, shape tip as for little finger. Index finger measures approximately 2¾ inches (6.9 cm).

THUMB:

Remove waste yarn; with Main Color (or color of choice), pick up 9 stitches from top and 9 stitches from bottom of opening, and distribute evenly on double-pointed needles; pick up 2 stitches from glove at each corner. Total: 22 stitches. Work as for little finger to the middle of nail, shape tip as for little finger. Thumb measures approximately 2½ inches (6.4 cm).

FINISHING:

Weave in ends neatly on reverse side. Steam block to even out stitches and obtain finished measurement desired.

Cunningsburgh Star

MAKER UNKNOWN

Here is a traditional Cunningsburgh Star—patterned cuff, fingers, and thumb with a star motif on the back—in a variation featuring a naturals color scheme with red highlights that really shine. The cuff has a snowflake pattern. I found this pretty pair in a shop in Cunningsburgh, Mainland.

KEY

- ■ Main Color - Maroon Heather
- ⊟ Maroon Heather - Purl on right side
- □ White
- ■ Black
- ▨ Beige
- ▨ Red
- ⊠ Chart B - work with Contrasting Color used on back of glove.
- ⊡ Chart B - work with Background Color used on back of glove.

CHART A Back of Hand

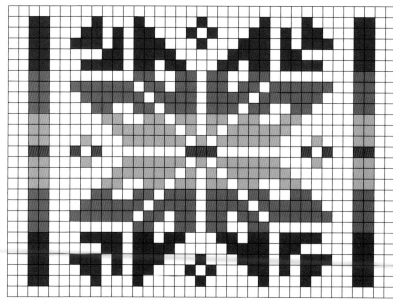

37 Stitch / 27 Round Repeat

Work Chart C (cuff); work Chart E (ribbing) for 2 inches; turn piece in-side out so that cuff will face right side when glove is completed; work rounds 1-5 of Chart D around entire glove; work Chart A on back of glove while working Chart B on palm; work rounds 5-1 of Chart D around entire glove. Follow finger/thumb Charts F and G for patterns and decreases.

CHART B Palm

4 Stitch / 4 Round Repeat

CHART C Cuff

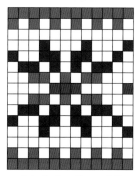

12 Stitch / 15 Round Repeat

CHART D Borders

4 Stitch / 5
Round Repeat

CHART E
Ribbing

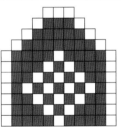 —Repeat this row
for length.
4 Stitch /
1 Round Repeat

CHART F
Thumb and Finger
Fronts and Decreases

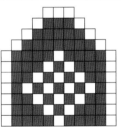

11 Stitch / 6 Round Repeat

CHART G
Thumb and
Finger Backs

4 Stitch / 4
Round Repeat

Cunningsburgh Star in Naturals with Hearts Gauntlets

MAKER UNKNOWN

This is a true Cunningsburgh Star glove with all naturals colors made with yarn from undyed fleece. It shows fine contrast between light and dark in a mixture of greys and browns. The cuffs, or gauntlets, as they are known in Shetland, have a peerie hearts pattern.

CHART A Back of Hand

2 Stitch/2
Round Repeat

CHART B
Thumb Gusset
and Palm

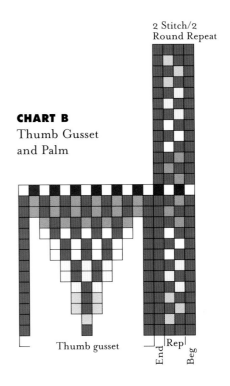

33 Stitch / 27 Round Repeat

Thumb gusset   End Rep Beg

CHART C Cuff

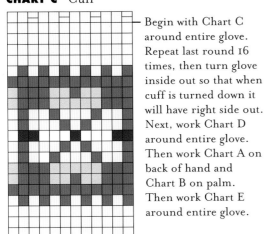

12 Stitch / 20 Round Repeat

Begin with Chart C around entire glove. Repeat last round 16 times, then turn glove inside out so that when cuff is turned down it will have right side out. Next, work Chart D around entire glove. Then work Chart A on back of hand and Chart B on palm. Then work Chart E around entire glove.

KEY

☐ Main Color - Beige

⊟ Main Color-Purl on Right Side

■ Dark Brown

☐ Lt. Grey

■ Black

▨ Charcoal

☐ White

Border Charts

CHART D

CHART E

Borders: Work Chart D around entire glove after Cuff, increase 2 stitches on back of hand on first round. Work Chart E around entire glove after completing Charts A and B.

CHART F Fingers/Thumb

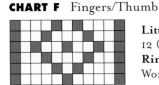

11 Stitch / 6 Round Repeat

Little (Middle) Finger: Work 12 (18) rounds, then Chart G.
Ring, Index Finger, Thumb: Work 18 rounds, then Chart H.

Shaping Charts

CHART G

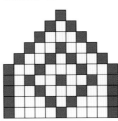

CHART H

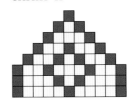

Work back of fingers and thumb in 2 stitch repeat, using the palm pattern and keeping edge stitches in brown as shown on Charts F, G, and H. Use beige and brown only.

Cuffed Cunningsburgh Star Variation

KNIT BY BARBARA ISBISTER

I found this treasure at the Sunday flea market in the Cunningsburgh community center. All the traditional elements of a Cunningsburgh star are combined with a truly wonderful non-traditional color scheme.

KEY

- ☐ Beige - Main Color
- ⊟ Beige - Purl on Right Side
- ☐ White
- ☐ Orchid
- ☐ Pink
- ☐ Deep Rose
- ☐ Fushia
- ☐ Light Grey
- ☐ Violet
- ☐ Light Pink
- ☒ Chart B - Use Contrasting Color used on back of glove.
- ☐ Chart B- use Background Color used on back of glove.

CHART A   Back of Hand

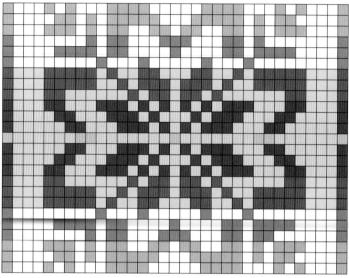

33 Stitch / 25 Round Repeat

CUFF: Work 4 rounds Chart E; then Chart D around entire glove, and turn work work inside out; work Chart E for 2¼".

GLOVE: Work 3 rounds Main Color; then Chart C around entire glove. Work Chart A on back of glove while working Chart B on palm in colors indicated, and rounds 1-15 of Chart F for thumb gusset. Work rounds 5-1 of Chart C around entire glove. Work rounds 16-36 of Chart F for front of thumb and fingers; then Chart B on back of thumb and fingers.

CHART B   Palm

2 Stitch / 2 Round Repeat

CHART C   Borders

4 Stitch / 5 Round Repeat

CHART D Cuff

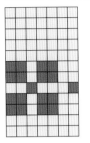

7 Stitch / 12 Round Repeat

CHART E Ribbing

3 Stitch Repeat

CHART F Thumb Gusset

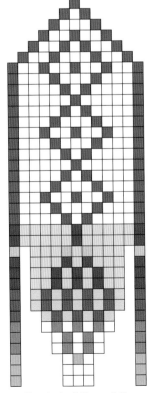

13 Stitch / 36 Round Repeat

Cunningsburgh Star Outline Variation

MAKER UNKNOWN

This variation of the Cunningsburgh Star pattern is the only one I've ever seen and I quickly snapped it up when I found it in a shop in Cunningsburgh. It features a simple color scheme and a spacious geometric look. What makes it so unique is that it's an outline-type glove filled in with lines instead of a solid color. Also the background color has taken the place of the pattern color.

CHART A Back of Hand

31 Stitch / 31 Round Repeat

After ribbing, work Chart A on back of hand while working Chart B on palm in colors indicated. Work fingers and thumb from Charts F and G as indicated.

Cuff

CHART C

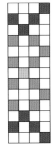

4 Stitch / 4 Round Repeat

CHART D
Border Ribbing

2 Stitch / 3 Round Repeat

CHART E
Middle Ribbing

3 Stitch / 1 Round Repeat

CUFF: Begin with Chart D, then Chart C. Turn inside out so cuff will face right side when glove is completed. Work Chart E for 2 inches.

KEY

☐ Main Color – Beige

⊟ Beige – Purl on Right Side

☐ White

▨ Taupe

▧ Gold

■ Brown

☒ Chart B – use Contrasting Color used on back of glove.

CHART B Palm

4 Stitch / 4 Round Repeat

Fingers and Thumb

CHART G Shaping

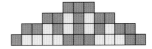

CHART F Thumb Gusset

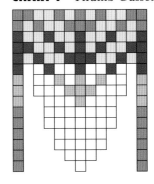

Using Taupe/Beige only, work finger front same as the thumb and work Chart B on back.

Traditional X's and O's

MAKER UNKNOWN

Found in Lerwick, this two-sided glove is in the traditional Norwegian style, but the colors are totally Shetland traditional. See the pattern for mittens in the Lerwick X's & O's project on page 23.

CHART A Back of Hand

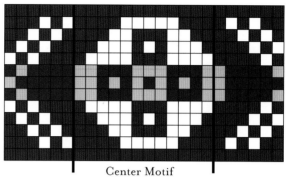

Center Motif
24 Stitch / 13 Round Repeat

CHART A1 Alternate Center Motif

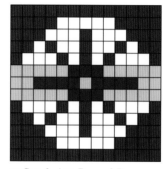

13 Stitch / 13 Round Repeat

CHART B Palm

2 Stitch / 2 Round Repeat

CHART C Border

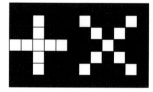

12 Stitch / 7 Round Repeat

KEY

- ▨ Main Color - Dk. Red
- ☐ White
- ▨ Dk. Brown
- ▨ Gold
- ▨ Navy Blue
- ⊠ Chart B - work with Contrasting Color used on back of glove
- ⊡ Chart B - work with Background Color used on back of glove.

After working ribbing, work Chart A, Chart C, then Chart A, [substituting Chart A-1 for center motif of second repeat], while working Chart B on palm in colors indicated. Continue in Main Color to length desired.

Traditional Allover

MAKER UNKNOWN

These specialty gloves from Mainland, called allovers, have been knit in the same design for at least fifty years, and are specific to Shetland. They are usually knit in very bright colors, such as this pair in yellow and brown. It's a difficult pattern to knit because of all the color changes, which requires very detailed stitching. See another version in the next project, Earth-tones Allover Variation.

CHART A Back of Hand

35 Stitch / 31 Round Repeat

KEY

⬛ Main Color – Dark Brown

⊖ Dark Brown – Purl on Right Side

▨ Brass

▨ Orchid

▨ Pink

▨ Lavender

▨ Peach

▨ Light Blue

☐ White

⊠ Chart B – use Contrasting Color used on back of glove.

Work cuff Charts C and D as indicated. Increasing 9 stitches across back of glove on first round, work Chart A on back of glove while working Chart B on palm and Chart E for thumb gusset; work Charts F and G for fingers and thumb.

CHART B Palm

4 Stitch / 6 Round Repeat

CHART C Cuff

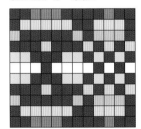

12 Stitch / 11 Round Repeat

CHART D Cuff Border

2 Stitch / 6 Round Repeat

CUFF: Work rounds 1- 6 of Chart D, then Chart C, then rounds 6 -1 of Chart D.

CHART E Thumb Gusset

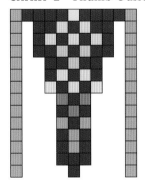

CHART F
Front of Fingers and Thumb

7 Stitch / 4 Round Repeat

CHART G
Back of Fingers and Thumb

2 Stitch / 2 Round Repeat

Earth-tones Allover Variation

MAKER UNKNOWN

Notice the unique contrast between muted and bright colors in this earth-tones version of the allover design. Like the pair of gloves on the previous page, this pair also came from Mainland.

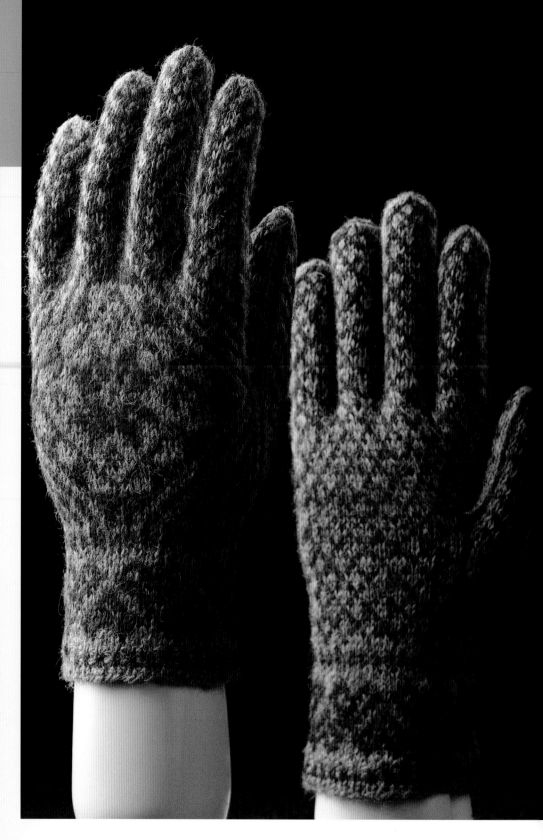

CHART A Back of Hand

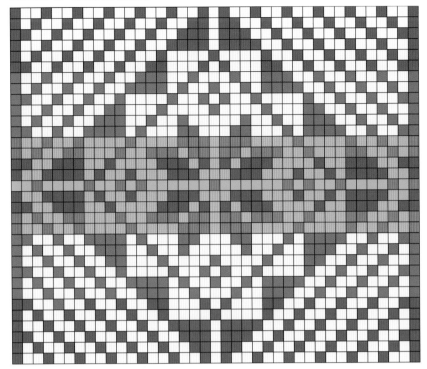

39 Stitch / 33 Round Repeat

KEY

☐ Main Color - Beige

⊟ Main Color - Purl on Right Side

■ Brown

▨ Tan

▨ Red Orange

▨ Medium Green

▨ Lime Green

4 Stitch / 4 Round Repeat

CHART B
Thumb Gusset/Palm

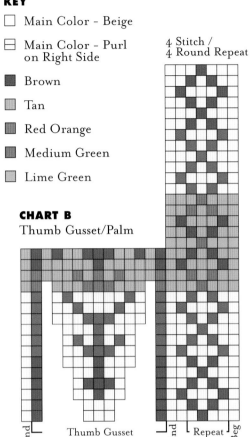

End ⌐ Thumb Gusset ¬ End ⌐ Repeat ¬ Beg

Fingers and Thumb

CHART D Front Shaping

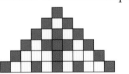

CHART E Front

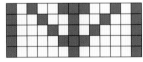

II Stitch / 4 Round Repeat

CHART F Back

End ⌐Repeat⌐ Beg

4 Stitch / 4 Round Repeat

GLOVE:

Work Chart C. Then work Chart A on back of hand while working Chart B on palm.

THUMB:

Front – continuing pattern from Gusset, repeat rounds 3-5 of Chart E.

Back – work 4 stitch repeats on Chart F; repeat rounds 2-5 for length.

FINGERS:

Front – work rounds 1-5 of Chart E; repeat rounds 3-5 of Chart E for length.

Back – continue 4 stitch repeat on Chart F; repeat rounds 2-5 for length.

BOTH:

Decrease as shown in Chart D, maintaining solid color edges on back and front.

CHART C Cuff

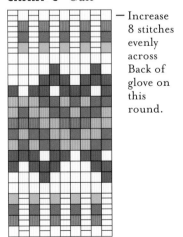

— Increase 8 stitches evenly across Back of glove on this round.

10 Stitch / 21 Round Repeat

Skuda in Red

KNIT BY MARGARET PETERSON

These gloves, with their intriguing asymmetrical, yet balanced design were knit by Margaret Peterson, who is a world-famous lace knitter from Muness, Unst. While on a trip to Japan, she received the inspiration for this design and named it after Skuda, a small isle off the coast of Unst.

CHART A
Back of Hand and Palm

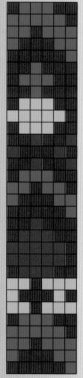

KEY

■ Main Color - Red
■ Dk. Green
□ Slate Blue
■ Navy Blue

Pattern is continuous around glove. After working Ribbing, work Chart A around entire glove.

6 Stitch / 31 Round Repeat

Skuda in Greens

KNIT BY MARGARET PETERSON

Here's another beautiful asymmetrical design inspired by Margaret Peterson's trip to Japan.

CHART A
Back of Hand and Palm

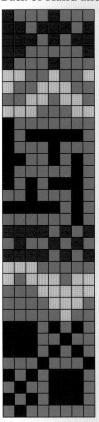

KEY

■ Main Color - Blue-Green

■ Navy Blue

■ Yellow-Orange

■ Bright Red

After working ribbing, work Chart A around entire glove.

8 Stitch / 34 Round Repeat

Traditional Star

MAKER UNKNOWN

Yell is a relatively sparsely populated island covered by peat bogs; however, it is the home of one of the earliest settlements in Shetland, known as the Old Haa. The main building in the settlement has been renovated and turned into the Old Haa Museum and Shop, where I bought these traditional star pattern gloves. The unknown maker left her signature in the red center stripes.

CHART A Back of Hand

27 Stitch / 27 Round Repeat

CHART B
Palm

4 Stitch / 2 Round Repeat

CHART C
Top Border

4 Stitch / 3 Round Repeat

CHART D
Bottom Border

4 Stitch / 5 Round Repeat

KEY

☐ Main Color - White
■ Dk. Brown
▨ Lt. Grey
▨ Taupe
▨ Red
⊠ Chart B - work with Contrasting Color used on back of glove.

After working ribbing, work Chart D and first round of Chart A around entire glove; continue Chart A on back of glove while working Chart B on palm; work last round of Chart A around entire glove; work Chart C around entire glove.

CHART A Back of Hand

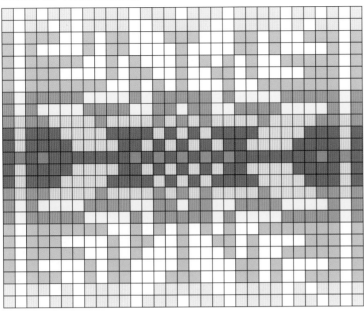

31 Stitch / 25 Round Repeat

MAKER UNKNOWN

Blue and yellow stars are popular motifs in Unst knitting. This pair of gloves has an interesting composite thumb gusset and a bright red center stripe. My friend Margaret Petersen sent them to me as a gift.

KEY

- ▨ Main Color - Light Blue
- ▢ Pale Blue
- ▢ Yellow
- ▢ White
- ▨ Medium Blue
- ▢ Light Yellow
- ▨ Navy Blue
- ▨ Peach
- ▨ Tangerine
- ⊠ Chart B - work with Contrasting Color used on back of glove
- ⊙ Chart B - work with Main Color used on back of glove.

After working ribbing, work Chart C around entire glove; work Chart A on back of hand while working Chart B on palm in colors as indicated; work rows 1-5 of Chart C around entire glove, continue in Main Color to length desired.

CHART B Palm

2 Stitch / 2 Round Repeat

CHART C Borders

2 Stitch / 5 Round Repeat

Whalsay Vertical Star

KNIT BY KATHLEEN SMITH

The Island of Whalsay is one of the smaller of the Shetland Islands. It's known for knitted garments with a very specific traditional style of vertical patterning. This particular type of richly all-over patterned glove, composed of vertical stripes and stars, is known as the Whalsay Star. The next project, Confetti Star, was also knit by Kathleen Smith.

RIGHT GLOVE: Begin palm as indicated, work 4 stitch repeat around; end as indicated.

LEFT GLOVE: Turn Chart, begin and end as indicated.

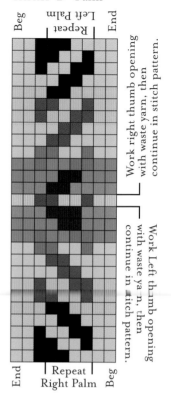

CHART B Palm

4 Stitch / 4 Round Repeat

KEY

- Navy - Purl
- Lt. Blue
- Navy
- Lt. Grey
- White
- Black
- Aqua
- Turquoise
- Maroon
- Dk. Periwinkle
- Lt. Periwinkle
- Dk. Green

CHART A Back of Hand

33 Stitch / 27 Round Repeat

CHART C
White Ribbing

4 Stitch / 4 Round Repeat

CHART D
Lt. Blue Ribbing

4 Stitch / 4 Round Repeat

RIBBING: Cast on with Navy; work rounds 1-4 of Chart D 3 times; work rounds 1-4 of Chart C once, then rounds 1-3 once, [7 rounds Chart C]; work round 4 of Chart D; then rounds 1-4 twice; then rounds 1-3 once.

CHART E
Fingers and Thumb

4 Stitch / 4 Round Repeat

CHART F
Fingers and Thumb Shaping

FINGERS AND THUMB: Work Chart E. Work shaping at tips according to Chart F.

CHART A Back of Hand

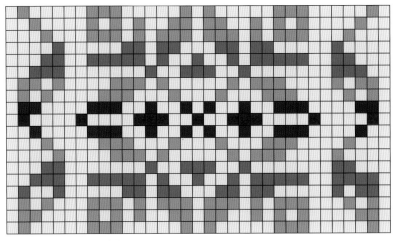

33 Stitch / 19 Round Repeat

CHART B Palm

4 Stitch / 6 Round Repeat

CHART C Top Border

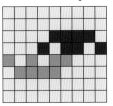

9 Stitch / 8 Round Repeat

CHART D Bottom Border

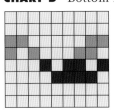

9 Stitch / 8 Round Repeat

KEY

☐ Main Color – Beige Confetti

▣ Teal

▪ Navy

▪ Green Heather

■ Brown

■ Red

☒ Chart B – Use Contrasting Color used on back of glove.

After working ribbing, work Chart D, Chart A, then Chart C on back of hand, while working Chart B on palm.

Confetti Star

KNIT BY
KATHLEEN SMITH

Kathleen Smith let her creativity triumph in this glove: an unusual small star with borders. The use of a confetti yarn, the shrinking and changing of the star shape, and the irregular borders are all unique to Kathleen's work.

Star Flower Variation

MAKER UNKNOWN

I call this pattern "star flower," for it combines elements of both shapes, and has become popular on all the islands. This glove from Mainland has a feature unusual in Shetland gloves—a hemmed cuff. The cuff is patterned, as in a Cunningsburgh Star style, but the fingers and thumbs are not. The color scheme is subdued but contrasting.

CHART A   Back of Hand

33 Stitch / 27 Round Repeat

KEY

- ■ Main Color - Dark Brown
- ▨ Taupe
- ▨ Grey
- ☐ White
- ▨ Bronze Heather
- ⊡ Yarn over
- ⊠ Knit 2 together
- ⊠ Chart E - use Contrasting Color used on back of glove.

CHART B   Palm

4 Stitch / 4 Round Repeat

CHART C   Fold Line

Fold line

CHART D   Cuff

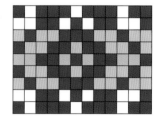

12 Stitch / 9 Round Repeat

CHART E   Border

4 Stitch / 7 Round Repeat

Work 2" Stockinette stitch (knit 1 row, purl 1 row); complete Chart C; work Charts D and E around entire glove. Work Chart A on back of glove while working Chart B on palm. Continue with Main Color around entire glove, if necessary, for length.

Open Medallions in Orange

KNIT BY KATHLEEN SMITH

Medallions with a complex pattern on the palms are one of Kathleen Smith's favorite patterns, but she never makes the same pair twice. This glove shows post World War II Norwegian influence in the use of two pattern bands on the back of the hand combined with geometrics on the palm. The next project is another of Kathleen's medallion-style gloves.

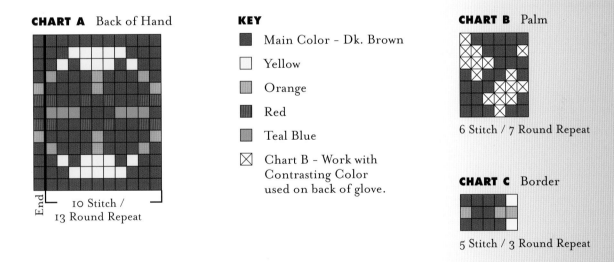

CHART A Back of Hand

End

10 Stitch / 13 Round Repeat

KEY

▪ Main Color - Dk. Brown

☐ Yellow

▪ Orange

▪ Red

▪ Teal Blue

⊠ Chart B - Work with Contrasting Color used on back of glove.

CHART B Palm

6 Stitch / 7 Round Repeat

CHART C Border

5 Stitch / 3 Round Repeat

After working ribbing, work 1 round Main Color around entire glove [first round of Chart A]. On back of glove work Chart A, Chart C, then repeat Chart A once while working Chart B on palm throughout, using colors indicated; work 1 round of Main Color around entire glove.

Filled Medallions in Bright Colors

KNIT BY KATHLEEN SMITH

Here's another of Kathleen Smith's medallion gloves. I requested the colors and she designed the pattern, based on medallions in pinks, lavenders, and blues on a silver background.

CHART A Back of Hand

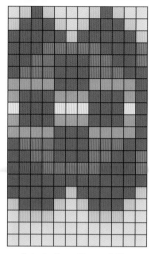

12 Stitch / 20 Round Repeat

After working ribbing, work rounds 1–20, then rounds 19–7 of Chart A on back of glove while working Chart B on palm; then work round 6 of Chart A around entire glove.

KEY

☐ Main Color – Silver Grey

☐ Light Blue

☐ Navy

☐ Magenta

☐ Fushia

☐ Pale Pink

☒ Chart B – work with Contrasting Color used on back of glove.

▢ Chart B – work with Background Color used on back of glove.

CHART B Palm

4 Stitch / 4 Round Repeat

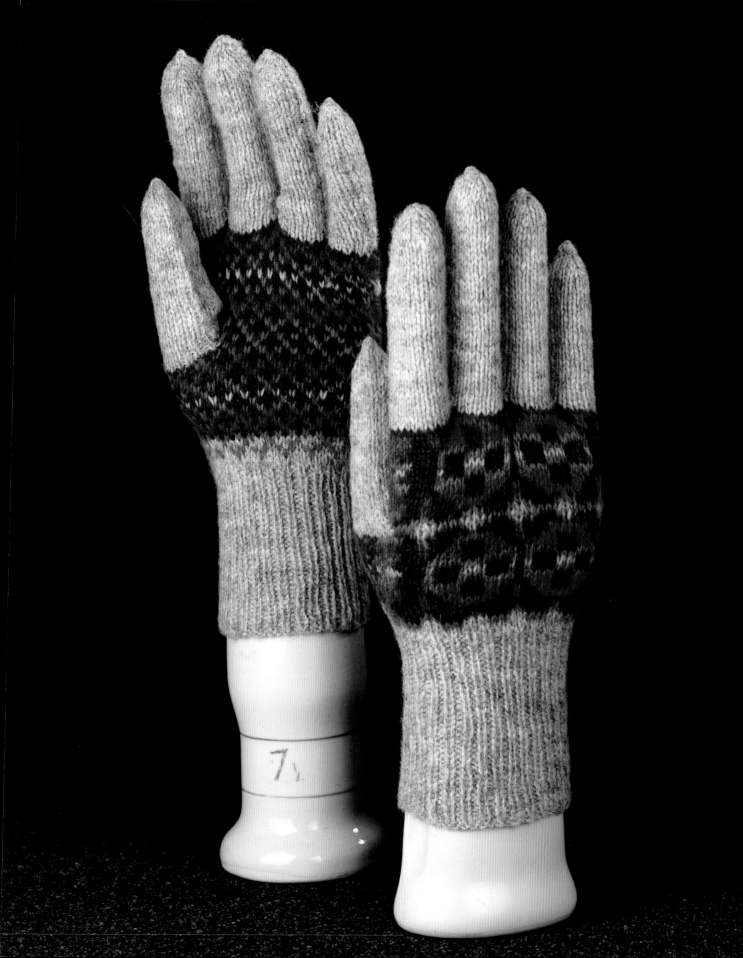

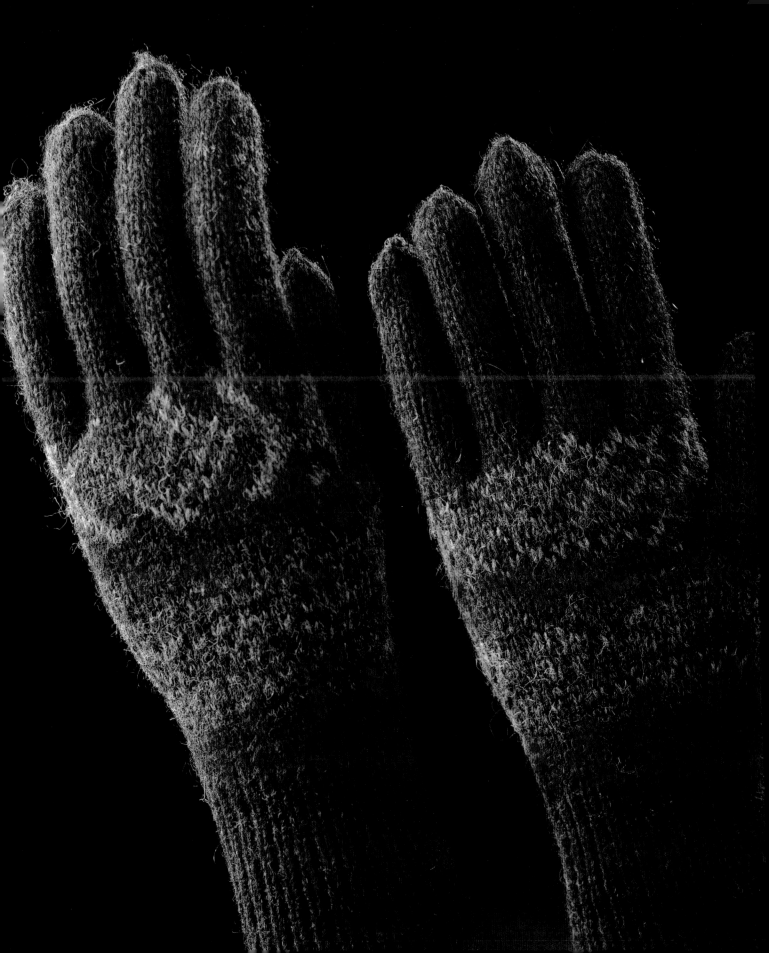

CHART A Back of Hand

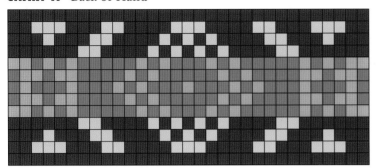

31 Stitch / 13 Round Repeat

KEY

 Main Color - Maroon Heather

Teal Heather

Light Teal

Bright Red

Orange

Chart B - work with Contrasting Color used on back of glove.

Chart B - work with Background Color used on back of glove.

After working ribbing, work Charts C, D, and E around entire glove; then work Chart A on back of hand while working Chart B on palm.

CHART B Palm

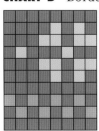

4 Stitch / 4 Round Repeat

CHART C Border #1

6 Stitch / 4 Round Repeat

CHART D Border #2

8 Stitch / 10 Round Repeat

CHART E Border #3

6 Stitch / 4 Round Repeat

Ruby Wine Composite

DESIGNED BY
WILMA MALCOLMSON

You can spot a Wilma Malcolmson glove a mile away. Here's a pair featuring one of her asymmetrical designs with patterned bands, some of which are circular, and some two-sided. Wilma usually avoids contrasting colors in her gloves, using instead many subtle heather shades, which give her gloves their characteristic look. "Ruby Wine" is her name for this color scheme. The next several projects were designed by Wilma or her mother.

Small Lozenge Star

DESIGNED BY
WILMA MALCOLMSON

Here's another of Wilma's unique patterns in the traditional style. Her design involves shrinking the star and bordering it with a patterned diamond. The colors are rich, dark, and subtle with plenty of light–dark contrasts.

CHART A Back of Hand

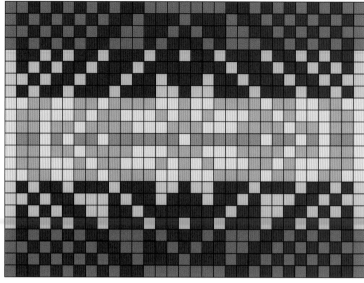

31 Stitch / 23 Round Repeat

KEY

- ■ Navy Heather - Main Color
- ■ Mahogany
- ■ Gold
- ■ Pale Pink Heather
- ■ Slate Blue
- ■ Light Mahogany
- ⊠ Chart B - Use Contrasting Color used on back of glove.
- ⊙ Chart B- use Background Color used on back of glove.

CHART B Palm

4 Stitch / 4 Round Repeat

CHART C Borders

4 Stitch / 6 Round Repeat

After working ribbing, work rounds 1-6 of Chart C around entire glove; work Chart A on back of glove while working Chart B on palm in colors indicated; work rounds 6-1 of Chart C around entire glove, then continue with Main Color for remainder of glove.

Large Hearts

KNIT BY MRS. FRASER

These stunning, although somber, two-pattern band gloves are another pair made by Mrs. Fraser, who has been knitting for more than 80 years. Note the lighter center border, which gives a feeling of space to the center of the glove.

KEY

- ☐ Natural - Main Color
- ▨ Dark Green
- ▨ Burnt Orange
- ☐ Brass Heather
- ■ Purple
- ▨ Beige

CHART A
Back of Hand and Palm

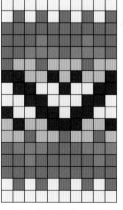

10 Stitch / 17 Round Repeat

CHART B
Border

4 Stitch / 2 Round Repeat

Pattern is continuous around glove. After ribbing, work Chart A, Chart B, then Chart A; work remainder of glove with Main Color.

Butterflies

KNIT BY MRS. FRASER

Butterflies are an old pattern, here rendered in a bright color scheme. The gloves have the traditional two pattern bands going all around and a muted center border for contrast. They were knit by Wilma Malcolmson's 93-year-old mother Mrs. Fraser, who lives in Mainland. See Butterflies for Bairns on page 49, for a version of the butterflies pattern made for babies.

CHART A
Back of Hand and Palm

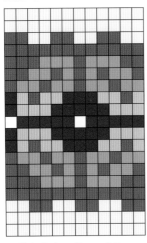

12 Stitch / 19 Round Repeat

KEY

☐ Natural - Main Color

◼ Mahogany

◼ Mauve

◻ Salmon

◼ Dark Red

☐ White

◼ Dark Mauve

CHART B

4 Stitch / 3 Round Repeat

Pattern is continuous around entire glove. After working cuff, work Chart A, then Chart B, then repeat Chart A. Work remainder of glove in Main Color.

CHART A Back of Hand

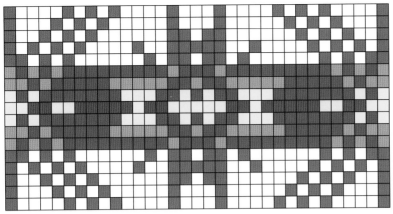

33 Stitch / 17 Round Repeat

Wilma's 1928 Star

DESIGNED BY
WILMA MALCOLMSON

The his glove is typical of the work of Wilma Malcolmson: an asymmetrical design that includes a separate back and palm motif, and some patterned bands that circle the glove. Wilma took this star design from a photograph of a sweater her mother knit in 1928.

KEY

☐ Black - Main Color

▨ Sage Green

▨ Slate Blue

☐ Yellow

▨ Dk. Green

▨ Red

▨ Gold

⊠ Chart B - Use Contrasting Color used on back of glove.

⊡ Chart B- use Background Color used on back of glove.

CHART B Palm

4 Stitch / 4 Round Repeat

CHART C Border #1

4 Stitch / 5 Round Repeat

After working ribbing, work Chart C around entire glove. Work Chart A on back of glove while working Chart B on palm in colors indicated. Work Charts C, then D, then C around entire glove.

CHART D Border #2

6 Stitch / 6 Round Repeat

Forest Cross

DESIGNED BY
WILMA MALCOLMSON

Wilma Malcolmson calls this color scheme "forest," to which I have added "cross." This design is characteristic of Wilma's work, showing low contrast and off-shades in heathers, which give the gloves a sophisticated, modern look.

CHART A Back of Hand

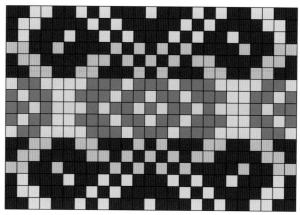

25 Stitch / 17 Round Repeat

KEY

- ■ Main Color - Maroon Heather
- ▨ Aqua
- ▨ Teal
- ▨ Pink Heather
- ▨ Tan
- □ Background Color
- ⊠ Contrast Color

CHART B Palm

4 Stitch / 4 Round Repeat

CHART C Borders

12 Stitch / 11 Round Repeat

After working ribbing, work Chart C around entire glove; work Chart A on back of glove while working Chart B on palm, using colors indicated; then repeat Chart C around.

Heather Lace Gloves

MAKER UNKNOWN

This lace glove in Fair Isle coloring is a specialty of Shetland. Virtually the only lace pattern now in use on gloves, it comes in a wide variety of related color schemes, which are always rich with Shetland's subtle shading. Because lace charts are complex, I thought it would be easier to understand the pattern if I just put it into words. To guide you while making these gloves, keep the photograph handy.

Follow the same finished measurements, materials, needles, and gauge instructions as in the Basic Women's Fair Isle Glove pattern on page 52.

PATTERN STITCH
(Multiple of 11 stitches)

Row 1: *Knit 3 (slip 1, knit 2 together, pass slipped stitch over); knit 3; yarn over. Repeat from * 5 times.
Row 2: Knit.

STRIPE SEQUENCE:

With Rust, purl 1 round, knit 2 rounds; knit 3 rounds Bronze; 2 rounds Teal; 2 rounds Tan; 2 rounds Peach; 2 rounds Rust. Purl 1 round Teal (thumb line); knit 2 rounds Rust; 2 rounds Peach; 2 rounds Tan; 2 rounds Teal; 3 rounds Bronze. With Rust, knit 2 rounds, purl 1 round.

After working ribbing with Navy, work stripe sequence in lace pattern around entire glove; continue in Navy for remainder of glove.

COLORS:
Navy Blue (Background Color), Bronze, Peach , Rust, Tan, Teal

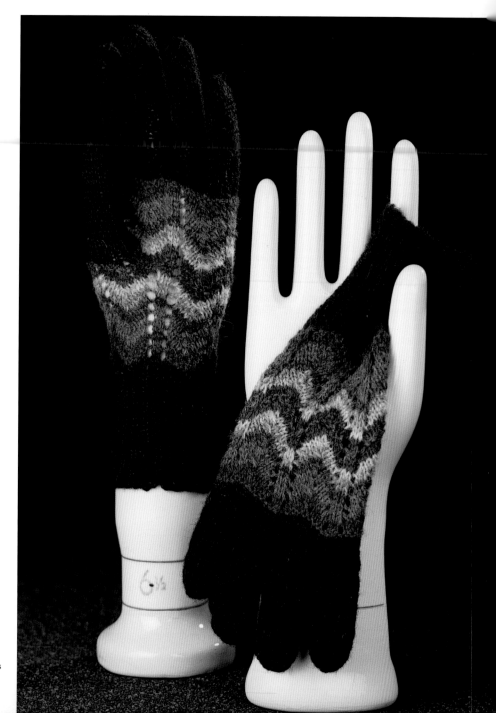

ACKNOWLEDGMENTS

I would like to thank all the Shetland knitters whose gloves and mitts appear in this book. Thank you to my friends Margaret Peterson and Kathleen Smith of Unst for teaching me the long needle/belt technique and for making sure that I learned it correctly. Margaret Peterson of Nor Nova Knitwear has also aided me in collecting gloves and information, and has eased my way into Shetland society.

Shetland knitter Mrs. Kathleen Smith and the author work together in Nor Nova, Unst.

My husband, Donald C. Noble, accompanied me to Shetland, took photographs there, helped to prepare the manuscript, and advised on many of the technical and editorial aspects of the book. Tommy Watt, curator of The Shetland Museum in Lerwick, generously allowed us to photograph gloves in the museum collection. Dee Neer did the graphics and Elly Osborne contributed to the manuscript preparation. Meg Swanson of Schoolhouse Press was a great help with materials, as were Jamieson & Smith Shetland Wool Brokers in Lerwick, Shetland. I greatly appreciate the support from my family and friends, with very special thanks to Margaret Dalrymple for her friendship, professional advice and continued support.

The author visits with Mrs. Johnson, from Baltasound, Unst, who has been knitting for more than 80 years.

BIBLIOGRAPHY

Allen, John, *Fabulous Fair Isle*. New York: St. Martin's Press, 1991.

Bunyan, Chris, and Mary Smith, *A Shetland Knitter's Notebook*. Lerwick: Shetland Times, Ltd., 1991.

Don, Sarah, *Fair Isle Knitting*. New York: St. Martin's Press, 1979.

Feitelson, Ann, *The Art of Fair Isle Knitting*. Loveland, CO: Interweave Press, 1996.

Fenton, Alexander, *The Northern Isles: Orkney and Shetland*. East Lothian, Scotland: Tuckwell Press, 1978, 1997.

Fryer, Linda F., *Knitting by the Fireside and on the Hillside: A History of the Shetland Hand Knitting Industry 1600-1950*. Lerwick: Shetland Times, Ltd., 1995.

Mowat, Farley, *The Farfarers—Before the Norse*. South Royalton, VT: Steerforth Press, 1998, 2000.

McGregor, Sheila, *The Complete Book of Traditional Fair Isle Knitting*. New York: Charles Scribner's Sons, 1981.

Nicolson, James R., *Traditional Life in Shetland*. London: Robert Hale, 1978, 1990.

Pearson, Michael, *Traditional Knitting*. New York: Van Norstrand Reinhold Co., 1984.

Rutt, Richard, *A History of Hand Knitting*. Loveland, CO: Interweave Press, 1987.

Starmore, Alice, *Alice Starmore's Book of Fair Isle Knitting*. Newton, CT: Taunton Press, 1988.

Turner, Val, *Ancient Shetland*. London: B. T. Batsford Ltd, 1998.

INDEX

Albans, 8
Butterflies patterns, 49, 89
Cunningsburgh Star patterns, 54, 56, 58, 60
Fair Isle style, 10-11
Fair Isle technique, 14-16
Fingerless gloves, 30-43
Fishermen's gloves, 42
Fishermen's mittens, 22
Glossary of Fair Isle knitting terms, 11
Gloves for babies, 50-51
Gloves for women, 52-94
Gloves from Lerwick, 23, 32, 36, 62
Gloves from Unst, 20, 24, 26, 28, 42, 68, 69, 74, 76, 80, 82
Gloves from Yell, 22, 37, 70
Gunnister, 9
Herring trade, 9
Hosiery trade, 9
Knitting belts, 14-15
Knitting needles, 14-16
Knitting tips, 17
Medallions patterns, 40, 80, 82
Mittens, for babies, 48-49
Mittens, for children, 44-47
Mittens, for women, 18-29
Muness Castle, 8
Norwegian resistance, 11, 18
Norwegian Star patterns, 26, 28, 72
One-handed method, 15-16
Shaping gloves and mittens, 16
Shetland map, 8
Shetland wool, 12-14
Taking a background stitch, 16
Taking a pattern color stitch, 16
Truck system, 9
Two-handed method, 15
X's and O's patterns, 23, 62